D1625861

HOOVER DAM

HOOVER DAM

THE PHOTOGRAPHS OF BEN GLAHA

Barbara Vilander   The University of Arizona Press | Tucson

First printing

The University of Arizona Press

© 1999 The Arizona Board of Regents

All rights reserved

Manufactured in the United States of America

04 03 02 01 00 99 6 5 4 3 2 1

Library of Congress Cataloging-in-Publication Data

Vilander, Barbara, 1958–

Hoover Dam : the photographs of Ben Glaha / Barbara Vilander.

p. cm.

Includes bibliographical references (p.   ) and index.

ISBN 0-8165-1694-4 (cloth: alk. paper)

ISBN 0-8165-1695-2 (paper: alk. paper)

1. Photography in engineering. 2. Glaha, Ben D., 1899–1970.

3. Hoover Dam (Ariz. and Nev.)—Design and construction—

Pictorial works. I. Glaha, Ben D., 1899–1970. II. Title.

TR702.V55 1999

627.82'09791'59022—dc21

99-6107

British Library Cataloguing-in-Publication Data

A catalogue record for this book is available from the British Library.

Frontispiece: Down to Bedrock, by Ben Glaha, 1932

To Scott,

without whom this book would not have been possible,

and to Chandler, Britten, and my parents,

whom I also love more than I can say

CONTENTS

ILLUSTRATIONS

All photographs are black-and-white gelatin silver photographs.
Photographs are by Ben Glaha unless otherwise noted.

ACKNOWLEDGMENTS

The road that led to the completion of this text began at the Museum of Photographic Arts in San Diego. While employed there, I was inspired to pursue my study of art history after watching the director, Arthur Ollman, give his insightful walks through the exhibitions. I decided that I, too, wanted a depth and breadth of art historical knowledge that would enhance my comprehension of the photographic arts. I then pursued a master's degree at the University of California in Davis, where Harvey Himelfarb was instrumental in assisting me to fulfill my desire to expand not only my knowledge of art history but also, particularly, my interest in the history of photography. With Harvey's encouragement, I continued my graduate studies at the University of California in Santa Barbara. While at U.C. Santa Barbara, I experienced the invaluable support, both personal and academic, of my adviser, Dr. Ulrich Keller. The culmination of my doctoral studies was my dissertation, from which this text is drawn. I deeply appreciate the guidance I received from my committee members, Dr. Beatrice Farwell and the late Dr. David Gebhard.

The success I experienced in researching my text would not have been possible without the help of a number of individuals. I would like to cite the following people from specific venues where I collected the majority of my information: Patricia Eames, Richard Fusick, and, particularly, Kenneth Heger at the National Archives and Records Administration in Washington, D.C.; J. Harwood at the National Museum of Natural History; Patti A. Hager and Pat Lynagh at the National Museum of American Art; William E. Worthington, Jr., at the National Museum of American History; Cristina Carbone and Carol Johnson at the Library of Congress; Marty Coffey, Debra Lange, Jennine Regas, and Roy Wingate at the Bureau of Reclamation in Denver; Eileen Bolger and Joan Howard at the National Archives and Records Administration in Denver; Don Westphal, for his sense of humor and knowledge, at the Bureau of Reclamation in Sacramento; Bill Sharp at Hoover Dam; David Horvath at the University of Louisville; Tod Ruhstaller of the Haggin Museum: Pioneer Museum & Haggin Galleries in Stockton, California; Leslie Calmes at the Center for Creative Photography at the University of Arizona; Nancy Emerson at the San Diego Museum of Art; Dennis McBride at the University of

Nevada, Las Vegas; and Mark Hayward, Museum of Science and Industry, Chicago. Especially heart-felt thanks go to Gene Hertzog, Carl Trulsen, Andy Pernick, Mary Timme, and, above all, Bethe Visick at the Bureau of Reclamation Office of Public Affairs in Boulder City.

Numerous other individuals also deserve my gratitude, including Hoover Dam tour guides Joan Northrop and Don Wall; Rupert Spearman, for his personal recollections of Ben Glaha; and Glaha's nephew, Wes Nell, for opening up to me both the home and the experiences working for the Bureau of Reclamation that he shared with his uncle.

George Rinhart particularly deserves my appreciation for making available to me his knowl-edge of Glaha's work, along with his collection of Glaha's personal letters and mementos. Brit Storey, Senior Historian for the Bureau of Reclamation, performed the invaluable task of reviewing the manu-script and providing me with his comments. I am extremely grateful for his time, expertise, and exten-sive effort. I also appreciate the manuscript commentary provided to me by the Bureau's Public Affairs Office in Boulder City.

I am, of course, indebted to the University of Arizona Press for electing to publish my manu-script. Former acquisitions editor at the Press, Amy Chapman Smith, exhibited objectivity and pa-tience. Former development officer Ken Bacher provided expertise and support well beyond his job description. Acting Director Chris Szuter, manuscript editor Alan M. Schroder, and copy editor Beth Wilson guided the manuscript through the final stages of editing and publication.

Here at home, my parents, Marjorie and Jim Forrester, have been unwavering in their encour-agement. Additionally, my good friend Anne Renaud has provided moral and edible support above and beyond the call of duty.

Finally, no "thank you" can adequately convey the appreciation I have for the support given to me by my husband, Scott Vilander, to whom this text is dedicated.

THE BACKGROUND

When visitors see Hoover Dam for the first time, its huge size invariably produces a visceral reaction. The monolithic structure, 726 feet tall and 660 feet wide at its base, can hold behind it in Lake Mead up to twenty-eight million acre-feet of water. The United States Bureau of Reclamation, in the Department of the Interior, built the dam from 1931 to 1936 to control the radically waxing and waning flow of water in the Colorado River. With a regularized flow, crops and structures alongside the river would be protected. Further, water channeled through the dam could be used to produce electricity.

The structure, however, was controversial. The dam was by far the largest of its type at that time and carried with it unexplored engineering risks. It also was to be constructed during the depressed economy of the 1930s. Bureau leadership was keenly aware of public and political reservations regarding the technical challenge and fiscal scale of the project. In order to provide evidence that the project was structurally sound and that government funds were being utilized wisely, the Bureau adopted an aggressive policy of making detailed photographic documentation of the dam's construction. Bureau employee Ben Glaha proved perfectly suited for the task.

Glaha's still photographs serve as technical documents of the micro and macro aspects of the construction process. The Bureau carefully released his images to legislators, the press, and the public in order to sell them on the project's importance and efficient management. What set Glaha apart from other photographers was his ability to produce images that could be utilized for technical documentation, propaganda, and fine-art exhibitions with equal effectiveness.

Glaha's artistic inclinations led him to create photographs of the construction process that were presented as fine-art images in museum and gallery exhibitions. Glaha was, as an employee of the Bureau, necessarily a propagandist. His personal penchant, however, was art. He cleverly dovetailed his vocation and his avocation by creating images that revealed in the construction site the formal beauty of line, shape, pattern, and texture.

In preparing this book, I located as many of Glaha's Hoover Dam construction photographs as possible. Fifty Glaha photographs are reproduced here. Their titles are the captions originally assigned to the images. Supportive materials in the form of Bureau correspondence and publications from the

National Archives and Records Administration were examined to determine why the photographic documents were initiated, when they were created, and how they were utilized. Glaha's nephew, Wesley Nell, was able and willing to supply what library and archive holdings could not: insight into the background and personality of Glaha himself. All of the materials gathered from public and private sources were considered within the social, political, and artistic climate of America in the early 1930s.

Hoover Dam remains one of the most significant public construction projects of the twentieth century. Since construction began, the dam has been a popular tourist site, currently drawing more than eight hundred thousand visitors per year. Public interest in the dam is usually centered on the facts pertaining to its construction. The dam's undeniably overwhelming physical presence has generated folklore as well. For example, divers checking the silt level at the upstream face of the dam supposedly encountered fish described as carp the size of Volkswagen Beetles; and the reason the water in Lake Mead is blue and the water exiting the dam from the powerhouse downstream is green is said to be that the interior of the intake towers was coated with yellow paint. Perhaps if Glaha had thought to don a diving suit, the photographic documentation of Hoover Dam might have included a colossal carp or two.

Until now, neither Glaha nor his Hoover Dam construction photographs have been given considered examination. Glaha and his images are worthy of such a discussion not only because of their subject matter but also because the technical/propagandistic and artistic dichotomy of Glaha's images is unprecedented in the work of a government photographer. Whereas in contemporary society, our voracious cultivation of celebrities leads to ready acclaim, in the 1930s a more anonymous work ethic prevailed. Further, Glaha did not seek public attention but was content to work steadily under the Bureau's aegis. As a result, it is not until now that one of the most significant figures in the photographic arts has been given the technical and creative recognition he is due.

HOOVER DAM

1

THE SHOVEL AND THE CAMERA

The Bureau Tames the Colorado

Hoover Dam, one of the most significant water resource projects in the West, is built in a remote desert canyon where the searing heat routinely pushes thermometer readings into the triple digits. At the time of its construction, it was the "largest building project in the western hemisphere following the completion of the Panama Canal."[1] The decision by the United States Bureau of Reclamation to erect such a monumental structure in the inhospitable environment of Black Canyon, thirty miles southeast of Las Vegas, did not come readily. The Bureau's determination was based on considerable research, including explorations and surveys of the area dating back to the mid-nineteenth century. Geological surveys of the Colorado River and its surrounding terrain indicated that with the introduction of water, seemingly inhospitable land could become habitable and even agriculturally profitable. However, in order to obtain that water, the fickle flow of the Colorado had to be harnessed. The repeated scientific surveys of the river, which attempted to explore, chart, and devise ways to regulate the Colorado, culminated in the Bureau's construction of Hoover Dam.

At the end of the Civil War, attention shifted from the civilized eastern coast of America to its unexplored western frontier. The Civil War had enervated the United States, psychologically and financially. With the war's end, people were eager to put behind them the sights and memories of its destruction and turn their attention to the virgin territories of the West. Private enterprises such as the railroads were no longer fiscally limited by the war and were eager to examine the untapped resources west of the Mississippi. There was, however, one impediment to the development of the far western territories: a severe lack of rainfall. The vast territories of what would become fifteen middle and western states of the Union received significantly less than the national average of thirty inches of rain per year. Yet the lure of land to be settled was greater than the existing climatic conditions, and individuals and teams of explorers set out to determine what lay west of the Mississippi.

While a few intrepid souls had ventured to the far West prior to the Civil War, more intensive exploration of the land came in the 1860s and 1870s. From 1867 to 1877, Clarence King led the U.S.

Geological Exploration of the Fortieth Parallel.[2] Cameras were integral tools of the exploration teams because photographs concisely conveyed the geographical, geophysical, and anthropological aspects of the frontier. Accompanying King as official photographer was Timothy O'Sullivan. O'Sullivan was well suited to the rigors of photographing while traveling with an overland survey because he had taken hundreds of outdoor wet-plate photographs during the Civil War. From 1870 to 1879, another well-known western landscape photographer, William Henry Jackson, traveled with Ferdinand V. Hayden's U.S. Geological and Geographical Survey of the Territories. Jackson's images are among the best examples of the power of western landscape photographs to influence public opinion about the West; his images of Yellowstone so impressed Congress that in 1872 the government declared it America's first national park.

More relevant to this study are the surveys that dealt specifically with the Colorado River region. The first documented investigation of the river occurred in 1858 when Lieutenant Joseph C. Ives attempted to sail up the Colorado from Yuma, Arizona, on a scientific mission. The first fifteen miles took him a week, and after his ship, the *Explorer*, ran aground, he ventured by skiff as far upriver as Black Canyon, the future site of Hoover Dam, before terminating his voyage.[3] In a much more thorough, government-sponsored project begun in 1869, Major John Wesley Powell, under the auspices of the Smithsonian Institution in Washington, explored the Colorado River basin over a period of three years.[4] Powell's extremely arduous and daring quest took him down the river "from source to mouth."[5] In the process of traveling eighteen hundred miles and running twelve hundred rapids, Powell christened the places he visited with such descriptive names as Hell's Half Mile, Echo Park, Separation Rapids, Black Canyon, and Boulder Canyon. By naming the various localities, Powell was laying claim to them as property of the United States government. Other expeditions, such as Lieutenant George M. Wheeler's 1871 survey west of the 100th meridian, also charted the Colorado River.

All these ventures on the Colorado produced the same conclusion: its waters were a force of nature not to be reckoned lightly. It alternately roiled and trickled as it passed through both narrow chasms and open vistas. It was impassable for commercial navigation. However, if regulated amounts of water could be diverted from the riverbed, there would be the potential to create and support civilian settlements. The question thus became how to harness the Colorado's enormous resource.

For many years, irrigation techniques were quite rudimentary, hardly going beyond the canal irrigation skills of the ancient Hohokam Indians. But gradually, technological innovations such as the steam shovel permitted the construction of irrigation projects of increasing complexity. The modest beginnings led developers to look for climates and terrain where they could employ their irrigation skills.

Southeastern California's Imperial Valley, with its temperate climate and large tracts of seemingly cultivable land, was a particularly appealing place to experiment with irrigation and crop cultivation. In 1901, Charles Robinson Rockwood's newly established California Development Company completed a canal that diverted Colorado River water sixty miles into the Imperial Valley. Fifteen hundred settlers had prepared land for planting and, thanks to the river's ability to turn desert into verdure, by 1904 the valley's population had increased to seven thousand. Those first four years of settlement, though, were deceptively quiescent years for the Colorado River; the river's rate and volume of flow were steady and predictable. However, in November 1905, the Colorado's water, augmented by a surge from the Gila River, suddenly raged unchecked into the Imperial Valley, transforming the Salton Sink into the Salton Sea. And in 1910 the river's sudden violence again rent its former boundaries, resulting in a $7 million congressional emergency flood control appropriation. By then it seemed that the river had, so to speak, people's attention. The solution, however, was not to abandon attempts to harness the river but to implement more stringent methods of control. The Imperial Irrigation District, a non-governmental organization, proposed the All American Canal, which would provide controlled diversion of river waters totally within U.S. boundaries. The canal proposal was defeated, however, largely owing to the efforts of Arthur Powell Davis. What is paradoxical about the canal proposal's defeat is that Davis was the director of the Reclamation Service, a newly formed government agency specifically chartered to reclaim arid lands for settlement and cultivation. Davis's reasoning was that the tremendous undertaking of regulating the Colorado's flow should be left not to private developers but to the federal government, specifically his Reclamation Service.

The Reclamation Service, operating under the aegis of the Department of the Interior, was created for the purpose of supplying the arid West with water resources. In order to approach such a broad challenge, a comprehensive irrigation plan had to be implemented. In 1891, in Salt Lake City, Utah, the problem was addressed by the National Irrigation Congress, an organization strongly supported by Theodore Roosevelt. Roosevelt felt that water development should fall under national jurisdiction, particularly in those instances where state and local groups did not have the means to implement large-scale projects. He envisioned federal water projects encouraging westward expansion, easing population pressures in the eastern United States, providing for water conservation, and aiding the agricultural economy.[6]

With the passage of the Reclamation Act on June 17, 1902, Roosevelt created the Reclamation Service, later renamed the Bureau of Reclamation. Dams, canals, and waterways were immediately proposed and approved for construction. The Bureau's mandate was to serve seventeen western states via water storage and management systems, and by 1911 eleven water storage facilities had been completed. Construction continued at such a rapid pace that by 1928, "Reclamation was acclaimed as the world's foremost builder of water storage, diversion and distribution systems."[7] The Bureau today remains one of the largest suppliers of water to the West.

In order to address the challenge of regulating the Colorado, Congress commissioned the Interior Department to make a comprehensive study of the Colorado River basin and the ramifications of its development. The result was the Fall-Davis Report, published in 1922 after three years of research. The report stated that the United States government should construct a giant dam "at or near Boulder Canyon" and recoup the cost of the project by selling electricity to burgeoning southern California.[8] Once a dam was completed and the river's flow was regularized, the All American Canal would be constructed. After some debate as to how to divide the waters diverted from the river, the Colorado River Compact was signed on November 24, 1922. Subsequently, the Boulder Canyon Project Act (also known as the Swing-Johnson Act, after its authors) was introduced in 1923. A revised version was passed on December 14, 1928, and on March 7, 1930, funds were approved for the dam's construction. Thus the United States government, specifically the Bureau of Reclamation, assumed responsibility for harnessing the Colorado River by means of a dam at Black Canyon.[9] A group of construction companies incorporated in Delaware on February 19, 1931, joined to submit a bid for the construction contract for Hoover Dam. In a reference to their half-dozen units—Utah, Morrison-Knudsen, J. F. Shea, Pacific Bridge, MacDonald & Kahn, and Bechtel-Kaiser-Warren Brothers—the group adopted the name Six Companies. The Bureau of Reclamation awarded it the contract on March 4, 1931.[10]

Seven western states stood to benefit from the regulation of the river's flow: Wyoming, Colorado, Utah, New Mexico, Arizona, Nevada, and California. In order to appropriate the assumed annual flow of at least eighteen million acre-feet, the seven states were placed into two divisions: Wyoming, Colorado, Utah, and New Mexico in the upper division, and Nevada, California, and Arizona in the lower division. Each division was to share in the water's flow, with individual states receiving specific amounts. Each state benefited in its own manner. For example, during World War II, California used electrical power flowing from the dam to produce fighters, bombers, and cargo planes for the war effort. After the war, electricity flowing from the dam supported southern California's aerospace industry.[11]

As of September 30, 1989, $20.9 billion "have been invested in Reclamation facilities," and the Bureau would like all of its efforts to be positively perceived.[12] Since the creation of the 1902 Reclamation Act, however, authors have criticized both it and subsequent Bureau legislation.

For example, in 1907 an article appeared in *Overland Monthly and Out West Magazine* in which the author criticized the Reclamation Act on the basis that there were private parties that had, prior to the Act, successfully irrigated and settled desert areas but "must submit to be robbed and lose their all simply because the Government could build a better system than they had been able to build with their limited capital."[13] In a 1989 publication, Doris Ostrander Dawdy found fault with the Reclamation Act. She maintained that had its authors incorporated the resources of the Geological Survey, the Corps of Engineers, and the Department of Agriculture, the combined knowledge of those organizations would have made for a far better Reclamation Service.[14]

The Geological Survey, for example, was able to classify lands as "arable, irrigable . . . having due regard to humidity of climate, supply of water for irrigation, and other physical characteristics."[15] More specifically relating to Hoover Dam, Dawdy indicated that in the Fall-Davis Report, which justified the construction of Hoover Dam, Arthur P. Davis, the Reclamation Service's director from 1914 to 1923 under Interior Secretary Albert B. Fall, "overestimated the Colorado River's potential for satisfying the needs of all the river-basin states and Mexico." In fact, Davis had disregarded the findings of E. C. LaRue of the Geological Survey, which contained relevant information regarding the Colorado's flow, amount of sediment, areas available for irrigation, and potential reservoir sites, as well as LaRue's conclusion that the Colorado "did not 'furnish enough water to irrigate all available acreage.'"[16]

Other authors have challenged the Bureau's decisions from an economic point of view. Richard Berkman and W. Kip Viscusi, for example, stated that although Bureau projects are intended to serve the public, the public monies spent by the Bureau frequently go for private gain. The Bureau, according to Berkman and Viscusi, justifies spending in the private sector by stating that project benefits for the private sector will make their way to the public and thus outweigh the public cost of the projects.[17] Further, they state that the Bureau's method of benefit-cost evaluation for each project virtually guarantees that the project will gain congressional approval.[18]

The Bureau's manipulation of financial and geological data has, according to Dawdy, nearly caused its own demise. She states, "The manipulations to obtain projects and the heavy deficits those projects generated so distressed Congress by the 1920s that it considered phasing out the reclamation program." Dawdy goes on to relate that what saved the program, ironically, was the depression of the 1930s, when it became advantageous to provide jobs for the unemployed.[19] The largest Bureau work site in the early 1930s was Hoover Dam.

The general public, conscious of the large allocation of government funds for the construction of Hoover Dam, and those knowledgeable regarding the legislative and political history of the project, looked for documentation, financial as well as visual, in order to gauge the efficacy of the Bureau's efforts. Since television, with its wide dissemination of visual information, was not commercially available when Hoover Dam was built, photographs in print media were the best means of relaying the methods and outcomes of Bureau projects. Just as photographs from the surveys almost half a century earlier had revealed the water resources, so images were now made to record the transformation of those resources into productive elements.

Additionally, the 1929 stock market crash and subsequent depression fueled the need for proof of purpose for any government project, especially one the magnitude of Hoover Dam. The government photographs produced during that time were careful to project an aura of economic optimism and efficacy. Pete Daniel and Sally Stein point out that Congress, in an effort to limit budgetary expense while increasing support for New Deal relief programs, sought to exert some control over 1930s government publicity. The outcome was a characteristic "documentary" style that, while appearing candid, "promoted the value of forceful, bureaucratic government intervention to shore up a stagnant economy."[20]

The government already had an established system for disseminating publicity; the Committee on Public Information, dating to World War I, had information officers and an organized publicity program. The system continued under the Hoover administration, when construction on the dam began, and into the Roosevelt administration, when the president targeted the dam as New Deal evidence of the nation's economic recovery. To further its New Deal programs, Betty Winfield states,

> the Roosevelt administration needed professional information officers who could formulate, dramatize, and communicate information for the departments. Since the success of the New Deal programs demanded the widest possible public support, the executive branch had to have an aggressive campaign of public information to advertise the agencies' services, to justify the bureaus' usefulness to the citizen, and to garner support from Congress.[21]

Since there were no televised press conferences, what more dramatic way to communicate progress than with published photographs? Further, governmental precedents existed for utilizing photographs for publicity. For example, the U.S. Department of Agriculture employed camera-made images in "transmitting images of progress."[22] Its visual publicity campaign produced twenty-three thousand images, which are now housed in the National Archives.[23] The photographic recording of the construction of the Panama Canal serves as an example of a long-term documentary project involving construction and water resource management. Beginning in 1907 and continuing for some twenty-three years, Ernest Hallen, the official photographer of the Isthmian Canal Commission, recorded all aspects of the program from its initial excavations, mosquito eradication, individual lock constructions, and support services such as bakery, laundry, and school to the final filling of the canal.[24] Thus, to promote the construction of Hoover Dam, the Bureau of Reclamation commissioned arresting photographs from the project site and presented them to the public and to other government branches. The goal was to garner project appreciation and support. How and why one Bureau employee, Ben Glaha, was appointed to make those images is the subject of the next chapter.

2 THE UNIQUE TALENTS OF BEN GLAHA SUIT THE TASK

Bernard Dean Glaha had a very diverse career prior to working as the Bureau of Reclamation's Boulder Canyon Project photographer; the variety of his hobbies and prior employments prepared him for the multiplicity of tasks he would accomplish while working at the dam. Regrettably, not a great deal of information is available regarding Glaha's personal life. He was, according to those who knew and worked with him, a very private person, not forthcoming with information about his life beyond the job site. The few facts ascertainable about his background and employment history can be gleaned from his personal correspondence and Bureau of Reclamation documents. Glaha was born March 2, 1899, in Kansas City, Kansas, to Bernard Glaha of Iowa and Catherine Murphy of Missouri. At his death on November 8, 1970, in Sacramento, California, he was survived by a sister, Winnie Obrecht of East Aurora, New York, and a brother, Jack Glaha of Thousand Oaks, California. There is no official indication that Glaha ever married.[1]

Glaha's personal correspondence indicates that in 1917, the year following his high school graduation, he was in the U.S. Army, working as a clerk with the Medical Detachment of the Forty-third Infantry Division.[2] He continued his work with the Medical Corps, writing in December of the same year that it was his job to take charge of soldiers "who come up on sick report."[3] The following year he was the personnel clerk for the Personnel Department of the Division Surgeon's Office of the new Fifteenth Regular Army Division.[4]

Glaha's letters from this period convey his continued passion for music. In high school he was co-composer of the music for the 1916 "Senior Farewell" song, and while in the Army he was the music coordinator and pianist for a minstrel show at the "Y."[5] Later, while working at Hoover Dam, he directed a "3–4 piece orchestra and others from time to time."[6] In an entertaining combination of his musical and writing talents, he composed an article, "Boulder City Boasts a Band," for the Bureau publication *The Reclamation Era*.[7] Glaha's long-standing love of music would eventually mingle with his photographic endeavors: "It is possible that my early musical studies have left their impression. As a matter of fact, I time my printing with a metronome. I find a speed midway in the allegro suitable for both contact and projection work and, incidentally, something of a soothing influence during this drudgery."[8]

The first mention of Glaha's interest in photography appears in his Army correspondence. In a 1917 letter his mother stated, "I hope you got your 'Kodak' and that you have a chance to use it."[9] It is not evident from the letter whether Glaha had any prior experience with a camera. By 1919, though, Glaha, who was still in the Army, was assigned to the Educational Section of the Reconstruction Department as a photography instructor.[10] In addition to his professional photographic work, he continued to send home snapshots of unidentified subjects.[11] In 1920, the newsletter for Camp Meade (Maryland) announced that Sergeant First Class Glaha, chief instructor in USGH Fort Sheridan Reconstruction School, would offer a course in photography.[12]

Glaha's army correspondence does not indicate when or why his service with the armed forces ended, but two pieces of evidence indicate that after his military service Glaha worked as a journalist: first, a 1924 letter sent to Glaha in care of the Fort Madison, Iowa, *Evening Democrat*, and second, a newspaper clipping from the *Evening Democrat* indicating that Glaha had worked for nine months as the paper's city editor and was then promoted to editor.[13] No information is available on the extent of Glaha's photographic activity during the early 1920s.

Glaha's work with the Bureau of Reclamation began on March 4, 1925, when he was hired as a timekeeper in Pavillion, Wyoming. From March 1925 until October 1926, Glaha worked as a chainman and recorder of surveys. There is a break in his employment with the Bureau from October 1926 to September 1930, at which time he was reemployed in Pavillion, Wyoming, as a senior engineer draftsman.[14] In 1931, Glaha began working on the Boulder Canyon Project in Designs and Drafting.

Examples of Glaha's earliest engineering activities on the project include his sketch of the new Administration Building and his assisting in formulating a plan to number houses and streets in Boulder City.[15] He also created a *Map of the Boulder Dam Area Showing the Principal Points of Scenic and Historical Interest*.[16] In 1931, the Bureau realized that there was a need for photographic documentation of the building of the dam. In April of that year, construction had begun, and by November the river had been diverted around the point where the dam would stand. The construction engineer at the project, Walker R. Young, found Glaha, with his variety of skills, to be a perfect fit:

> We have planned that the organization should include a photographer, but we doubt if the duties would consume the entire time of one man, and for that reason it is planned to utilize the services of B. D. Glaha, Senior Engineer Draftsman, for this purpose. Mr. Glaha while rated as a draftsman would more nearly qualify as an artist than the average. He is able to sketch and color pictures in a very satisfactory manner and in addition has had considerable experience in photographic work. He is intensely interested in this type of work and has an engineering background which is necessary to obtain the pictures of most value to the Bureau. He has served as an instructor in a photographic school in a signal corps during his army service and is

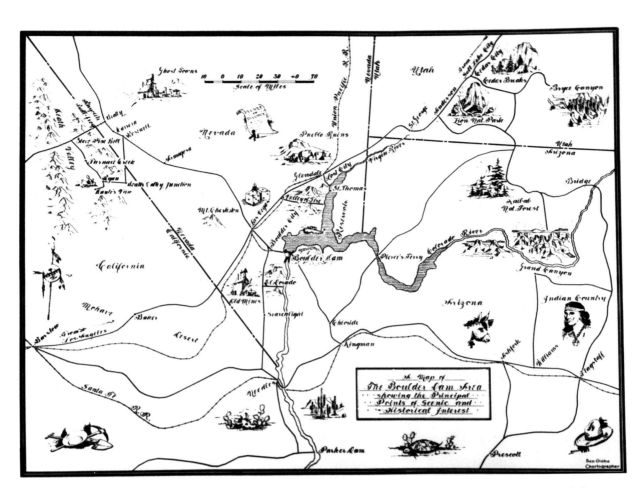

Map of the Boulder Dam Area Showing the Principal Points of Scenic and Historical Interest. Undated drawing.

well versed in the theoretical problems of photography besides having an eye for the proper arrangement of his subjects. He has taken a considerable number of the progress pictures and is familiar with most types of cameras including the ordinary movie outfit. . . . If his services in this connection do prove satisfactory, a combination of photographic work and drafting will be a happy solution.[17]

Thus it was that Glaha's drafting skills, combined with his photographic skills acquired in the Army, led to his position as Bureau photographer of the Boulder Dam Project. Because, as Young stated, the Bureau did not believe a full-time photographer was necessary, Glaha initially functioned as a draftsman while taking pictures on the side: the 1931 Boulder Canyon Project–Hoover Dam organization chart listed him under Designs and Drafting, with "Photographs" in parentheses after his name. The organization chart for the following year, however, indicates Glaha's expanding photographic role. Though he is again listed under Designs and Drafting, the title "Photographer," in parentheses, follows his name. By 1933 he was listed under the separate category of Photography, where his name remained until he transferred to the Bureau's Central Valley Project in 1936.[18]

What is highly significant in terms of this study is that Glaha was uniquely motivated to create photographs that would satisfy the technical needs of the project engineers by recording every step of the building process, and would function as news and aesthetic documents as well. As a result, his images appeared in such diverse venues as newspapers, trade and art magazines, government and commercial pamphlets, slide lectures, and commercial and art exhibitions.

Technically, Glaha's work is comparable to the efforts of other government and scientific photographers. And, aesthetically, his images are similar to the industrial photographs of artists like Lewis Hine and Charles Sheeler. Signed Glaha images were sold by the Bureau at higher prices than unsigned pictures, and his photographs found validation as art items in museum exhibitions.

Glaha was able to cross the line between art and record because of his technical background; his awareness of the sociohistorical context in which his images were created, including Bureau purpose and policy in image-making; and his own aesthetic abilities and aspirations.

Glaha's photography experience in the Army, combined with his understanding of engineering principles, enabled him to systematically secure photographs of all aspects of the dam's construction, from the embedding of sensors in the concrete to panoramas of the erection process. His understanding of the micro and macro engineering aspects of the dam's construction, gained through his work as one of its draftsmen, was critical to his ability to produce images that would illustrate graphically, to professionals and the public alike, how the structure was assembled. Trade publications, such as *Electrical West* and *Compressed Air Magazine*, used his images to illustrate technical articles, while *Life* and *U.S. Camera* selected images of more popular interest. Technically and artistically his images still stand today; for example, at the dam site his construction images are used for reference by engineers in maintaining and modifying the dam, as well as to entertain and edify tourists.

Glaha was aware of the sociohistorical climate in which he was producing his images, and that awareness functioned on two levels. First, he was cognizant of the fact that the construction of Hoover Dam was a record-breaking event. Statistics, such as the fact that without an internal cooling system it would take more than one hundred years for the concrete to cool, were relatively tame in comparison with the unfounded rumor that the dam was being constructed on an earthquake fault and would collapse at the slightest tremor. Further, the dam was being built during one of the worst periods of the American economy. While most of the funds for the project had been allocated prior to the Depres-

Ben Glaha. Bureau of Reclamation.

sion, all eyes were on the Bureau for validation of the massive expenditure of public monies, particularly those allocated by the Roosevelt administration. Glaha's images had to address the dam's physical stability and the public outcry for proof of financial efficacy. Second, the Bureau's "party line" was to produce images that addressed structural and monetary concerns, and to do so in a subtle fashion; photographs had to answer questions posed about the project while being careful not to incite further criticism. Images that stressed productivity, safety, and thrift were the order of the day. Instead of images of labor strikes, injury, and loss of human life, Glaha provided photographs of the speed and skill with which the project was being completed. In fact, the Bureau frequently sought to forestall any criticisms about the project by keeping the public and government sectors inundated with images of an efficient operation that was ahead of schedule. Glaha understood the Bureau's parameters and worked within them, yet at the same time he was able to interject his own creativity.

Glaha's personal criteria would not allow him to produce photographs that merely captured the technical aspects of the construction program. Instead, he sought to find artistic compositions in all aspects of the dam's fabrication. By all accounts he was a well-read individual with a taste for fine food, music, and art. He was a devotee of the work of Charles Sheeler and was acquainted with several renowned art photographers of the day, among them Ansel Adams and Margaret Bourke-White, with whom he shared an appreciation for the prevailing Machine Aesthetic. Adams gave a lecture on Glaha's work in conjunction with an exhibition of Glaha's images at the M. H. DeYoung Museum in San Francisco. The photographer Willard Van Dyke wrote a glowing article about Glaha's Hoover Dam imagery, praising his ability to take potentially mundane industrial scenes and imbue them with aesthetic life, thereby reflecting the Machine Aesthetic.

The Bureau took a proactive stance in regard to Glaha's display of his Hoover Dam images in artistic contexts such as museums. As long as their image labels indicated that the photographs were taken in relation to a Bureau project, Glaha was free to exhibit them. The Bureau's reasoning in allowing Glaha to display his images in artistic venues was that the exposure was positive publicity for the Bureau and for the project. As a result of their mutual understanding, a symbiotic relationship developed between Glaha and his employer. Glaha, for example, requested increased responsibility in developing and printing images from the project that might later appear in a public art venue, newspaper, trade journal, or popular magazine, thereby further promoting the Hoover Dam Project.

Finally, we turn to the photographic equipment Glaha used. His cameras and accessories are mentioned here because in some instances they, or the lack of them, determined the types of photographs he was able to make. For example, in November 1931, when Glaha was first asked to be a part-time photographer, he helped compile a list of camera equipment desired for use at the dam site. Among the items requested were a 5" x 7" Speed Graphic camera, an 8" x 10" Eastman view camera, and a Taylor-Hobson-Cooke telephoto lens for use with the Speed Graphic camera.[19] Only the Speed Graphic was approved for purchase.[20] It is surprising that such a basic piece of equipment as a telephoto lens would be denied, especially given the strength of Construction Engineer Walker Young's argument on its behalf: "Because of the depth of the canyon and the almost vertical slopes, a large amount of the details in pictures of the canyon wall stripping and similar work will be lost without such a lens. It is anticipated that camera points will be established for progress pictures, and these must of necessity be at a considerable distance from the work in progress because of the topography."[21] Commissioner Elwood Mead, however, did not feel that the telephoto lens would be used frequently enough to justify its purchase. Thus, initially, a 5" x 7" Speed Graphic was used to produce standardized 6.5" x 8.5" images.

Construction Engineer Young, however, most likely on Glaha's behalf, continued to lobby for a telephoto lens. He couched his argument in terms to which he thought Washington would be most likely to respond—a telephoto lens could result in sensational images not otherwise obtainable: "Because of the height of the canyon and the width at the top, there are a large number of views which it is impossible to get with an ordinary camera because of inaccessibility. For instance, no pictures have been possible showing the scaling of the canyon walls by the Six Company Employees. This work is highly spectacular and if properly photographed would make interesting subjects."[22] There is no correspondence extant that indicates whether the lens was purchased; further, no telephoto lens was listed in a May 1936 inventory of equipment at the photo lab in Boulder City.[23] Given that there appears to have been no telephoto lens in Glaha's arsenal, in all likelihood he placed himself at personal risk to obtain some of his images.[24] A wide-angle lens was also requested and, like the telephoto lens, is missing from the inventory.

Whenever possible, Glaha tried to surmount equipment obstacles. For example, when he decided to send Commissioner Mead five enlargements of images he had taken on the dam site, he fashioned his own enlarger from equipment he had on hand.[25] Glaha may have intended the images as a personal statement about his abilities and his belief that the Boulder City photography lab was capable of more than forwarding 6.5" x 8.5" prints and their negatives to Washington.

Glaha was also inventive when it came to photographing in low-light situations. Six Companies was quite impressed with the fact that he was able to capture the tunnel-lining operations with "smokeless flash powder" (it had experimented with flashbulbs, which failed to provide enough illumination, and ordinary flash powder, which created too much smoke). As a result, Glaha successfully produced Bureau images of which Six Companies requested copies.[26]

Over the course of his work on the project, Glaha did acquire more equipment, including cameras, lenses, tripods, printing and enlarging equipment, and laboratory equipment, even if it was not exactly what he would have preferred. A May 1936 inventory lists a 5" x 7" Eastman view camera with an f.6.8 Turner-Reich convertible anastigmat in Ilex universal shutter, a 5" x 7" Graflex with an f.4.5. Kodak anastigmat, a 5" x 7" Korona view camera without lens, and a 5" x 7" Kodak anastigmat lens f.7.7.

3 THE BUREAU'S USE OF GLAHA'S PHOTOGRAPHS

In the 1930s in the United States, government and industry alike employed images and text to convince the public of the efficacy of their projects. From the Department of Agriculture to the Otis Steel Company, documents were selected and presented in such a fashion as to make people want to know the nature and successes of public and private organizations. Likewise, carefully chosen Glaha photographs were presented to the American public by the Bureau of Reclamation as proof of Hoover Dam's structural and financial stability. To ensure proper attribution to the Bureau, the photographs were stamped on the back, "Please give credit if reproduced to: Bureau of Reclamation."

Before examining the types of images Glaha secured of the project, it is important to discuss the nature of documentary expression at that time, particularly the influence exerted on the Bureau by the executive branch of the U.S. government. I am not differentiating here between image and text, for two reasons. First, photographs were used as documents extensively during the 1930s.[1] Second, photographs were consistently used integrally with text.[2] Summarizing the documentary genre in the 1930s, William Stott breaks the category down into two components: "Human documents show man undergoing the perennial and unpreventable in experience, what happens to all men everywhere. . . . Social documentary, on the other hand, shows men at grips with conditions neither permanent nor necessary, conditions of a certain time and place. . . . One might say that a human document deals with natural phenomena and social documentary with man-made."[3]

Utilizing Stott's definition, and given that Hoover Dam was a man-made phenomenon, Glaha's work falls under the heading of social documentation. Stott states that social documentation tends to advocate social improvement. Such is the case with Glaha's work; it was an attempt, on behalf of the Bureau, to show the public that the dam's construction would improve the quality of life for people living downstream by controlling flooding and by providing a reliable source of irrigation water and electricity. Additional commentary on the nature of documentary photography by Roy Stryker, best known for his coordination of the Farm Security Administration photography unit, further defines the 1930s nature of the genre. Stryker embraced the belief that documentary photography comprised two major elements, "reality and emotion."[4] Although Stryker's two components may seem incompatible, art historian Ulrich Keller points out that for Stryker, viscerally presenting data meant that "information could be animated without losing or distorting its factual substance."[5] Stryker's position, that truthful information could be offered in such a fashion as to make it more digestible, if not enticing, was typical of 1930s documentation. The mandate for providing alluring photographs of the dam's construction came from the Oval Office.

Carefully coordinated releases of information were part of the overall public relations efforts of both Herbert Hoover's and Franklin Delano Roosevelt's administrations. While the most deliberate slanting and broad dissemination of information regarding Hoover Dam occurred during Roosevelt's presidency, public relations efforts regarding the dam began during Hoover's tenure. The Roosevelt administration, for example, revived a public relations program coordinated by the World War I Committee on Public Information.[6] The program had already been expanded during the 1920s, to the extent that the Hoover administration was spending more than $3 million on handouts alone.[7]

The Roosevelt administration, in the effort to promote its New Deal, so thoroughly dictated the materials reaching the news media that "By March 1935, one correspondent was remarking acidly that reporters now seldom wrote their own stories but had become mere messenger boys running between the government bureaus and their own offices carrying statements prepared by press agents."[8] Under Roosevelt's administration, the chain of command for gathering Hoover Dam information for public release began with the president and his information officer, Steve Early, who in turn looked to Secretary of the Interior Harold L. Ickes. Ickes garnered information from Dr. Elwood Mead, Commissioner of Reclamation in the Department of the Interior.[9] Mead corresponded directly with Construction Engineer Walker R. Young, at the dam site. As an example of the relay and approval of information, when President Roosevelt asked Secretary Ickes to preside over the dedication ceremony at Hoover Dam, Steve Early and the president both reviewed Ickes's speech prior to the event.[10]

Because the overriding concern in Washington was to be kept fully informed regarding the construction developments at the dam site and in Boulder City, photographs were used extensively to convey, first to Washington, then to the public at large, the progress being made. Commissioner Mead stated, "We want the world to know what is going on there and for that purpose, nothing is as effective as a good picture."[11] All negatives, along with completely titled, attributed, and dated prints, were to be sent to Washington. Hugh A. Brown, Director, Reclamation Economics, stated, "This will permit us to keep in close touch with the progress of development and enable us to obtain far greater publicity concerning the work than could possibly be the case locally."[12] There is no doubt that Bureau officials in Washington had greater access to people and publications anxious to assist in promoting the Bureau's efforts. However, by having all the negatives sent to Washington, the Bureau also gained the ability to screen out those images it did not wish to be publicized. The policy of sending all photographs to

Washington implies that Glaha was allowed free rein during his photographic efforts, and his images were censored only after having been completed. For the most part that was the case. The specific images Glaha made were not dictated by "shooting scripts" so long as they provided an adequate summary of the construction progress.[13]

The idea of a shooting script can be traced to the motion picture industry, where the director decides, prior to filming, precisely what scenes will be shot. Shooting scripts were used extensively in still photography work, for example, by photographers working for *Life* magazine and the Farm Security Administration. The use of shooting scripts usually meant an editor predetermined the manner in which a photographer approached an assigned subject.[14] The fact that Glaha did not appear to have been given shooting scripts indicates that there was a tacit understanding between him and the Bureau regarding what types of images were required. He, in turn, was given free rein to secure those images. In fact, Glaha was not even confined to working at a set time of day or a set number of hours a day. If he did not, for example, arrive on the site until noon and then worked until midnight, no one objected.[15] Glaha did at times provide the Bureau with his own proposed programs, but they read more as updates of his upcoming schedule than queries for approval.[16]

The Bureau did, on occasion, propose specific images or attempt to dictate what was photographed. For example, when the Bureau's chief photographer from Washington, D.C., George A. Beyer, was planning to visit the project to record the progress at the dam with both still and motion pictures, Hugh A. Brown wrote ahead to Walker Young, "I shall appreciate it if you will let me know approximately when you expect to have the landscaping completed, the trees and shrubs set out, and the town in general tidied up so as to afford the best photographic effect."[17] Commissioner Mead commented, regarding Beyer's visit, "If you can put on any 'stunts' to make a more effective presentation of what you are doing I shall very much appreciate it."[18] Presumably Glaha was likewise guided as to when might be the most advantageous time to take certain photographs, or that some images might contain more dramatic appeal than others. He seems to have understood and accepted his role within the organization: to present the Bureau and its efforts to the best possible effect.

The spectrum of topics upon which Glaha focused his camera was remarkably broad. In terms of rough categorization, they were overall views over time of the rising of the dam from Black Canyon, technical construction details, specific work routines, support equipment and machinery, milestones in the dam's construction, the town of Boulder City, the filling of Lake Mead, and images of everyone from visiting dignitaries to the on-site staff. (An additional group of images taken by Glaha were intentionally artistic and were meant to be displayed within the context of art photography. That aspect of his work is discussed in Chapter 4.)

Glaha's overall views of the building process serve as a good introduction to how the dam's construction took place. Overall images of the dam site were particularly important in illustrating, by juxtaposing sequential images, the dam's dramatic rise from the riverbed. The high canyon walls, cableway control tower, and catwalks provided several vantage points from which to photograph the construction. *Black Canyon Prior to Boulder Dam Construction*, taken from the Nevada canyon wall downstream of where the dam would eventually stand, shows the Colorado River flowing unimpeded through the canyon. *The Dam as Seen from the Control Tower of the 150-Ton Cableway* illustrates how, once the Colorado was flowing through the diversion tunnels in the canyon walls, the pouring of concrete in blocks and columns began. The upstream cofferdam, which guided the river into the diversion tunnels, leaving the construction site dry, is visible in the upper left-hand corner of the image. The downstream cofferdam (not visible) prevented the water, once diverted, from backing up into the dam site. *The Downstream Face of the Dam and a Portion of the Power Plant* shows the nearly completed vertical face of the dam and the reinforcement structures for the U-shaped powerhouse abutting the base of the dam and extending downstream along each canyon wall. Finally, the *Horizontal View of Downstream Face of Boulder Dam and Power Plant* shows the essentially completed dam and powerhouse. The valves release water not routed through the power plant. The water instead passes directly from the intake towers through penstock pipes in the canyon walls and into the river below. The image was taken from a permanent camera station near the lower portal road.[19] That camera station was utilized throughout the construction of the dam and is still employed for periodic photographs of the dam.

Many of Glaha's overall images concentrated on the downstream face of the dam in order to capture its rising vertical face. He also photographed the upstream face and, in one instance, created a panorama including the dam and Arizona and Nevada spillways. For example, *Boulder Dam as Seen from a High Point Upstream on the Arizona Rim of Black Canyon* serves to highlight the rapid rate at which the construction progressed. In that image, the dam and intake towers are completed and water has begun to fill Lake Mead. Photographs such as these were widely circulated by the Bureau because they served to bring construction developments to life and thereby generate public and government interest in the progress of the project.

Glaha also photographed technical construction details, such as a test to determine the consistency of a batch of concrete and the installation of the grouting system. Further examples of Glaha's construction detail photographs include one of the wall joints of the Nevada spillway tunnel and *Detail of Roof Slab and Beam Reinforcement in Canyon Wall Valve-House Structure*. In the latter, Glaha used his hat to provide a sense of scale. The technical construction detail photographs were intended primarily for in-house use by Bureau engineers. They appeared in Bureau technical reports and occasionally in specialty periodicals produced for the engineering and construction trades.

Along the same line as Glaha's images of technical construction details were his photographs

Black Canyon Prior to Boulder Dam Construction. Ben Glaha? From an old print.

The Dam as Seen from the Control Tower of the 150-Ton Cableway on the Nevada Rim of Black Canyon. December 30, 1933.

The Downstream Face of the Dam and a Portion of the Power Plant as Seen from the Low-Level Catwalk. Top Forms on Dam at Elevation 1,055. October 2, 1934.

Horizontal View of the Downstream Face of Boulder Dam and Power Plant with Discharge from Two Eighty-Four-Inch Needle Valves in Nevada Canyon Wall Valvehouse, from Permanent Camera Station near Lower Portal Road. April 13, 1938.

Boulder Dam as Seen from a High Point Upstream on the Arizona Rim of Black Canyon. Note Arizona observation point at left. December 5, 1935.

of specific work routines. Some very interesting things can be learned from the work routine pictures. For example, the problem of getting the men to and from their job sites in the canyon gorge was solved by building a perilous-looking, nearly vertical lift, seen in *Workmen Ascending Downstream Face of Dam on Skip Operating over Skids*. Images like the skip photograph complied with the prevailing social documentary mode of combining reality and emotion. The challenge of transporting concrete into the canyon was solved by a system of cables spanning the riverbed from which buckets with an eight-cubic-yard capacity were lowered. One of the buckets is shown in *Eight-Cubic-Yard-Capacity Concrete Bucket Discharging Load in Dam Column Form*. The gigantic buckets could be lowered precisely where needed, and their contents were discharged by the waiting workmen. In locations where the eight-cubic-yard buckets were too large to fit a confined space, smaller transit mixers were utilized. Glaha photographed a transit mixer in action in *Four-Cubic-Yard-Capacity Transit Mixer Discharging Concrete*. Once the concrete had been poured, it was compacted with compressed-air vibrators.

The Babcock and Wilcox Company set up an on-site manufacturing plant to construct the steel pipes used in the dam's appurtenant works. Plant workmen formed and finished the pipes, which were then lowered into the canyon via the cableways. Glaha photographed both a worker detailing a pipe section in the plant and the placement of a completed section of pipe in *Chipping Backing-up Strip on Thirteen-Foot-Diameter Pipe Section* and *Handling Thirty-Foot-Diameter Steel Penstock Pipe by Cableway*.

The most dramatic illustration of how a construction task was completed was exemplified by the high scalers. Through millions of years, the volcanic rock of the canyon had been split, pitted, and cracked by wind, water, and temperature variations so that sections of the walls, ranging in size from pebbles to boulders, threatened to fall on the men working below. "A pebble dropping a thousand feet could split a man's skull like a cleaver going through a ripe melon, and one of the bigger, automobile-size boulders falling on a work crew would have the same deadly effect as an exploding fragmentation bomb."[20] It was the task of the high scalers, seated in bosun's chairs suspended by ropes over the canyon wall and using jackhammers and crowbars, to locate and remove any potentially hazardous unembedded rock. In *Drillers at Work on Canyon Wall above Power Plant Location*, the perilous positions of the high scalers added a dash of the heroic and dramatized one specific work routine. The drama of the high scalers' task is echoed by the risk Glaha took to secure the image. Loaded with his camera equipment, he was lowered over the canyon wall to procure the photograph.[21]

In addition to the images of men working on the dam, Glaha took photographs of the project's support equipment and machinery. The control tower of the 150-ton cableway provided a bird's-eye view of the construction site. From the tower the cableway operator oversaw the lowering of materials into the canyon. Cranes were utilized in areas inaccessible by the cableways. The twelve-ton-capacity

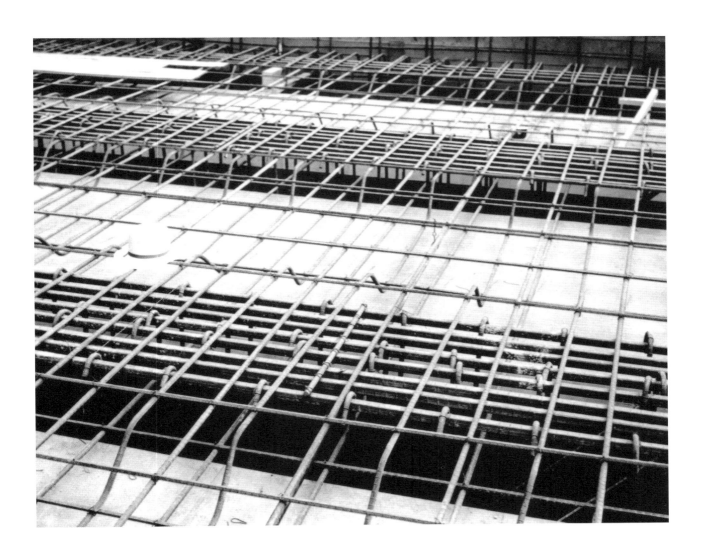

Detail of Roof Slab and Beam Reinforcement in Canyon Wall Valve-House Structure. June 1, 1935.

Workmen Ascending Downstream Face of Dam on Skip Operating over Skids. March 16, 1934.

Eight-Cubic-Yard-Capacity Concrete Bucket Discharging Load in Dam Column Form. The workman with a shovel in the lower right has just released the safety hook on a bucket. September 27, 1933.

Four-Cubic-Yard-Capacity Transit Mixer Discharging Concrete in Base of Downstream Nevada Intake Tower.
This view shows restricted conditions due to the close placement of reinforced steel. November 5, 1933.

Chipping Backing-up Strip on Thirteen-Foot-Diameter Pipe Section, Babcock and Wilcox Plant. October 23, 1933.

Handling Thirty-Foot-Diameter Steel Penstock Pipe by Cableway for Placement in Upper Nevada Header Tunnel. This view shows a bend section for installation below an intake tower being lowered over the rim of Black Canyon. Note the man sitting in the pipe. August 22, 1934.

Drillers at Work on Canyon Wall above Power Plant Location. April 10, 1933.

crane erected by the Lidgerwad Manufacturing Company, for example, handled the concrete and building materials for the Nevada intake towers and outlet tunnel raises. Two concrete plants were erected on-site. The first, low-mix, was positioned on a niche in the Nevada canyon wall and provided the cement for the diversion tunnel linings, the powerhouse foundation, and two-thirds of the dam. The second plant, high-mix, shown in *Cement Blending and Concrete Mixing Plants*, produced the concrete for the remainder of the construction.[22]

As concrete cures, it generates heat. If that heat were to remain, the concrete would expand, and then, upon cooling, would make the dam unsound. In order to displace some of the heat produced, pipes to contain chilled circulating water were laid throughout the dam. A refrigeration plant provided the cooled water for circulation. Once the concrete temperature was sufficiently reduced, the pipes were filled with grout and became part of the dam's reinforcement.

In addition to the daily work of the employees and support equipment and machinery, Glaha recorded certain milestones in the dam's construction. For example, the placing of the first million cubic yards of concrete in the dam was celebrated in *The Millionth Cubic Yard of Concrete Is Placed in the Dam Forms*. Also commemorated was the arrival of a Union Pacific streamliner on its first visit to the dam. Other photogenic moments were manufactured, such as the "stunt" when members of the Boulder Dam Consulting Board and officials of the Bureau of Reclamation and the Babcock and Wilcox Company were suspended in a pipe section over the Boulder Dam power plant, recorded in *Members of the Boulder Dam Consulting Board and Officials of the Bureau of Reclamation and the Babcock and Wilcox Company in a Thirty-Foot-Diameter Penstock Pipe Section*. No doubt a perk for the individuals involved, the image was not without its public relations intent.

Glaha was not only the project photographer; he was also expected to document Boulder City. Glaha's city photographs add another intriguing social documentary aspect to his work. When he turned his camera on Boulder City, it was to record the almost miraculous transformation of an arid plot of desert into a verdant, homey town. Such images are in keeping with Stott's belief that social documentation tends to advocate social improvement; the creation of the town advertised in microcosm the Bureau's ability to take seemingly uninhabitable land and transform it into a productive, lush habitat. The focal point of the town plan was the Government Administration Building and its attendant Escalante Plaza, seen in *Looking Northward across Escalante Plaza*. In a closer view, *Government Administration Building, Boulder City*, Glaha carefully framed the structure, with particular emphasis on the greenery in the upper left and lower right corners, to highlight the verdure of the setting. *North Section of Boulder City* reveals the juxtaposition of the grassy, cultivated landscape with the surrounding naturally arid terrain. Further Boulder City images by Glaha covered other amenities, such as government residences and the Boulder Dam Hotel, which was operated under government permit.

Cement Blending and Concrete Mixing Plants. Before 1935.

The Millionth Cubic Yard of Concrete Is Placed in the Dam Forms at 1:30 P.M. on January 7, 1934. Left to right: Chas. A. Shea, Director of Construction, Six Companies; Felix Kahn, Treasurer, Six Companies; Walker R. Young, Construction Engineer, Bureau of Reclamation; "Woody" Williams, Asst. General Superintendent, Six Companies; John C. Page, Office Engineer, Bureau of Reclamation; Frank T. Crowe, General Superintendent, Six Companies. January 7, 1934.

Members of the Boulder Dam Consulting Board and Officials of the Bureau of Reclamation and the Babcock and Wilcox Company in a Thirty-Foot-Diameter Penstock Pipe Section over Boulder Dam Power Plant. January 15, 1935.

Looking Northward across Escalante Plaza with Government Administration Building and Dormitory No. 1 Seen on Hill in Background. October 19, 1933.

Government Administration Building, Boulder City. A view from the southeast. October 21, 1933.

North Section of Boulder City Showing Parked Area as Seen from Water Tank Hill. July 27, 1934.

Inseparable from the construction of Boulder Dam was, of course, the filling of Lake Mead. As the lake began to form, land that had been above water disappeared from view. On more than one occasion, Glaha left the dam site and explored the areas that had been prepared for flooding. The Mormon farming town of St. Thomas, Nevada, for example, was deserted in preparation for the lake's formation. Glaha photographed *Abandoned and Dismantled Homesite at St. Thomas, Nevada*, as well as a cemetery from which the graves were to be relocated. Near St. Thomas was Pueblo Escondido, or Lost City, where a prehistoric Indian culture had been re-created. At Pueblo Escondido, Glaha recorded a restored kiva, or underground ceremonial chamber. In addition to photographs of specific sites that would be covered by water, Glaha recorded panoramas of the landscape prior to its dramatic alteration by the formation of the reservoir, for example, *View Looking Northeasterly across Reservoir Site from Observation Point.*

The water accumulating behind the dam would eventually create a lake that at capacity would be 115 miles long and extend 15 miles into the then "virtually unvisited" lower end of the Grand Canyon. In November 1935, Glaha took advantage of the rising reservoir to journey via boat over the waters of the forming lake. Previous trips overland into the Grand Canyon had been extremely difficult and therefore were made by only a few individuals. Now, traveling by water, Glaha secured photographs through which he meant to proclaim a newfound scenic heritage and to emphasize the harmony of nature and engineering.[23] The rock formation called The Sentinel, located at the lower end of the Grand Canyon, marked the entrance to the geological wonders ahead. Like the nineteenth-century explorer-photographers who marveled at the phenomena of Yellowstone and Yosemite, Glaha found impressive sites, such as a towering waterfall. Not only did Glaha reveal the daytime beauty of the lower end of the Grand Canyon, he also studied it under nocturnal conditions, producing *Late Evening View at the Lower End of Grand Canyon near Pierce's Ferry.*

Finally, to record some news images, Glaha photographed visiting dignitaries and occasionally the on-site staff. The most prominent visitors to the dam were Presidents Hoover and Roosevelt. In November 1932, Hoover made a brief inspection of the dam that was to become his namesake. Roosevelt dedicated the dam on September 30, 1935, at which time Glaha recorded *President Roosevelt Delivering Dedication Address.* While visits by such high-profile individuals were relatively rare, many people of very diverse occupations and interests came to tour what was being touted as the engineering marvel of its day. For example, Glaha was there with his camera when General Satumindo Cedillo, Minister of Agriculture of the Republic of Mexico, made an inspection tour of the dam in December 1935. Likewise, he photographed a group of engineering students from the University of Mexico who visited the project. The arrival of a Boy Scout troop and of a Shriners' convention band were also recorded as part

Abandoned and Dismantled Homesite at St. Thomas, Nevada. May 13, 1934.

View Looking Northeasterly across Reservoir Site from Observation Point. February 26, 1935.

Late Evening View at the Lower End of Grand Canyon Near Pierce's Ferry. November 7, 1935.

President Roosevelt Delivering Dedication Address. September 30, 1935.

of the dam's social history. In addition to visitors, Glaha made some group shots of the on-site Bureau staff to be placed in annual reports.

It is interesting to compare a few Hoover Dam construction images taken by Six Companies with related photographs taken by Glaha. The comparison reveals a certain conservatism on the part of Glaha versus the frankness of the Six Companies' photographer.[24] The Six Companies' images selected for comparison appeared in the book *So Boulder Dam Was Built*, by George Pettitt.[25] Copyrighted by Six Companies, the publication was meant to, and did, function as propaganda for the corporation. Yet even Walker Young felt Pettitt's text had a ring of authenticity to it: "Pettitt got the atmosphere of the job as no other writer has, to my way of thinking. . . . It is a form of propaganda but nevertheless it is interesting."[26] What is surprising about the book is that its text and photographs openly depict the inherent dangers at the dam site. One of the undated photographs in the book, for example, shows a truck on fire, with the caption "It doesn't take much to start fires at 128 degrees in the shade." Nowhere in Glaha's images is there such a dramatic example of the extreme conditions and resultant hazards everyone faced on the dam site.[27]

In those instances where there are somewhat comparable photographs by Glaha, his images are considerably less dramatic. For example, the Six Companies' image depicting the problem of keeping service vehicles on the roads—captioned "Keeping automotive equipment on the roads was not an easy task"—is a spectacular photograph in which two vehicles have plunged off an embankment, most certainly resulting in severe injury to their occupants. A Glaha image of a vehicular mishap, *The 200-Ton-Capacity La Crosse Trailer Used in Transporting Pipe Sections from Plant to Dam Slips*, is considerably less sensational. Likewise, when Six Companies depicts riggers working on a cable, the angle selected by the photographer frames the cable lines in such a manner that they converge on the worker on top of the cable while also emphasizing the height at which he is working and the deadly plunge into the canyon he and his assistant would make in the event of an accident. In a somewhat similar image, *Riggers on Boom of Twelve-Ton Crane at Nevada Intake Towers*, Glaha minimizes the danger inherent in high-elevation cable work. He frames the photograph so that the viewer cannot readily determine the height at which the men are working and indicates that the cable lines are securely attached to a crane. Moreover, Glaha's composition is an aesthetically appealing arrangement of geometric components.

Based on these examples, it appears that Glaha was considerably less sensationalist in his manufacturing of imagery than was the Six Companies photographer. Glaha's emphasis on safety and his avoidance of reference to mishaps were more than likely owing to unwritten Bureau of Reclamation policies prohibiting references to hazards and accidents. Six Companies was a private construction

Truck Burning. Unattributed.

Wreck of Cars at Nevada Spillway. Unattributed.

The 200-Ton-Capacity La Crosse Trailer Used in Transporting Pipe Sections from Plant to Dam Slips on Superelevated Roadbed between Boulder City and the Babcock and Wilcox Company Plant. July 16, 1934.

Cableway. Unattributed.

Riggers on Boom of Twelve-Ton Crane at Nevada Intake Towers. September 28, 1933.

conglomerate, while the Bureau was a government entity. The implication is not that Six Companies was careless concerning the safety of its employees. Rather, whereas the Bureau would remain liable to a tax-paying public, Six Companies, as a private enterprise, could afford to be more frank about the inherent dangers of the construction process. Neither organization could afford to overdramatize the dangerous aspects of the project; however, because the Bureau intended to manage such endeavors in the future, it had an increased motivation to portray the construction process in the most positive light possible. Based on his imagery, it is apparent that Glaha understood the Bureau's position and worked to satisfy the party line.

Art historian Karal Ann Marling's research sheds further light on why the Bureau, and therefore Glaha, avoided images that could have been construed as unflattering in any way. Although her research addresses federally commissioned post-office murals from the mid-1930s through the 1940s, she, like Glaha, was examining a government-sponsored project meant to be greeted with popular approval. She found that the Depression-era murals, "By showing long chains of events leading up to the present, historical cycles calmed public apprehensions of imminent catastrophe. . . . [H]istory chugged along placidly and predictably toward tomorrow."[28] And Glaha, in depicting the largest post–Panama Canal construction project in the Western Hemisphere, also was calming public concerns about the safety and monetary aspects of the project. He was showing, and the Bureau was thereby publicizing, the long series of construction tasks that led to the completion of the dam. The implication of that series was that the dam, by being well planned and executed, would naturally reach a safe and economical conclusion.

The broad range of photographs that Glaha took during the dam's construction was in keeping with the general nature of documentary expression at the time and with the specific needs of the Bureau of Reclamation. The images he produced answered any Bureau need for visual evidence, from technical data to public relations. A complementary aspect of Glaha's images is his creative response within the confines of the dam site.

4

MACHINE AESTHETIC
The Photographs as Art

In the years immediately following World War I, the nature of photography and the intentions of photographers changed dramatically. Photographs appearing on the pages of sophisticated European magazines literally reflected new perspectives. The images presented bird's-eye and worm's-eye views of previously unexamined subjects, such as industrial machine parts and impersonal glimpses of quixotic street scenes "that might have been collected by a mobile eye nervously scanning the surfaces of contemporary life."[1] The *neue Optik* (new vision), incorporating everything from X-ray images to cameraless pictures (images made by placing objects on photographic paper, exposing the paper to a light source, and developing the paper with photographic chemicals), was born of and reflective of a twentieth century that was rapidly becoming more technologically oriented.

The invention of elevators, skyscrapers, radios, and assembly lines, along with other engineering feats, marked a shift away from rural advancements to increased focus on urban development. Indeed, by 1927, owing to the benefits of advanced technologies, America was at its zenith in productivity and standard of living. Historian Thomas P. Hughes saw in this time period a world re-creating itself: "The development of massive systems for producing and using automobiles and for generating and utilizing electric power, the making of telephone and wireless networks . . . reveal the creative drive of engineers, industrial scientists, managers, and entrepreneurs possessed of the system builder's instincts and mentality. . . . The system builders, like [Henry] Ford, led us to believe that we could rationally organize the second creation to serve our ends."[2] Further, Hughes felt that the inventors and developers were responding to one of our most elemental desires: "Although the inventors, engineers, industrial scientists, and system builders created order, control, and system, in so doing they responded to a fundamental human longing for a world in which these characteristics prevail."[3]

In the 1920s and 1930s, an increased emphasis on mechanization led to a shift away from humanistic concerns. Judith Gutman wrote: "Where we had always been able to pinpoint the center of industrial life and see that a person occupied that same spot, we could no longer do that. . . . A person wasn't there. A machine was."[4] Indeed, people no longer looked to themselves for fulfillment in their lives; rather, they looked to their machines.[5]

In 1922, the photographer Paul Strand responded to the increasingly mechanistic spirit of his time by declaring that through the scientist/inventor a new technological Trinity had emerged: "God the Machine, Materialistic Empiricism the Son, and Science the Holy Ghost."[6] Strand's comment, in declaring that God was not humanistic but mechanistic, was the transcendent abdication of authority from man to machine. Other artists, like Strand, also felt the demission of human endeavor. As aesthetic interpreters of their time, they began to explore the machine and its relation to creative expression. Specifically, they employed the camera to express their own inventive impulses, and in so doing, they wedded themselves physically and intellectually to the Machine Aesthetic. Richard Guy Wilson concisely summarized this turn of events: "The choice of photography as the controlling and recording element is a particularly apt one: for the true artist of the machine age it was not enough to portray the impact of the machine or make it a symbol; he must himself become a machinist and utilize the machine as technique."[7]

The camera, as a machine, was deemed by artists to be an appropriate tool both to reflect and to reconstruct the modern world. The artist Raoul Hausmann opined about the artist's vision and the new society: "Why don't we paint works today like those of Botticelli, Michelangelo, Leonardo or Titian? Because our spirits have utterly changed. And not simply because we have the telephone, the airplane, the electric piano, and the escalator. Rather because above all these experiences have transformed our entire psycho-physiology."[8]

In order to express this newfound mental and physical transformation, architects, writers, and visual artists perceived a critical quality in the camera. They embraced its inherent capability to record whatever appeared before it in a seemingly direct and precise manner. Terms such as *sachlich* (objective, factual) and *neue Auge* (new eye or new perception) dominated the period.[9] The Russian photographer Alexander Rodchenko derided the established rules of standing erect and peering into the viewfinder at traditional subjects. The traditional style, which Rodchenko derisively referred to as "belly button" photography, was cast aside in his pictures of pine trees in Pushkino Park. He photographed the trees not from a distance but close-up, crouching on the ground quite near their bases or lying down amid them and pointing his camera directly upward. His perspective allowed the trees' elongated forms to rise directly above him like the view one has when standing at the base of a skyscraper and gazing toward its top.[10]

American art photographers who utilized the camera to explore the Machine Aesthetic include Charles Sheeler, who in 1927 and 1928 documented the activities of the Ford Motor Company's

River Rouge plant; Margaret Bourke-White, who recorded the workings of the Otis Steel Company factory and later, beginning in 1930, published those images and others like them in *Fortune* magazine; and Lewis Hine, who throughout the 1920s and into the 1930s sought to depict men at work with machines.

Glaha's being influenced by the Machine Aesthetic is directly traceable to his appreciation of works of art by Bourke-White, Hine, and, in particular, Sheeler. Regarding Sheeler, Glaha stated, "If anybody ever gets ART into a photograph there's the lad who will do it."[11] Sheeler's contact with European photographic trends was established by his inclusion in the Deutsche Werkbund's Film und Foto international exhibition in Stuttgart (May 18–July 7, 1929). Sheeler visited the exhibition and doubtless found there inspiration and affirmation of his style.[12] So enthusiastic was Sheeler about the power and grace of the new mechanistic depictions that he was moved to state, "Our factories are our substitutes for religious expression."[13] Glaha and Sheeler shared iconographic similarities in the depiction of technological structures. Moreover, both artists sought to stylistically reduce whatever they depicted to the essence of its function. The beauty in Sheeler's paintings and photographs, like the photographs produced by Glaha, came from the removal of all nonessential elements. Glaha once commented that the reduction of the subject to its absolute essence was a technique he had learned from the drafting process. He transferred this quality to his photographic work:

> Now engineering drawings, unlike architectural renderings, are never pictorial. Often drawings of this type do not even resemble the object represented. If they do depict the object directly, they do so with the least practicable number of lines and in the most direct manner possible. . . . However, drawings of this type are often beautiful. Whatever beauty they possess is not the result of superficial ornamentation of the drawing itself nor is it the beauty of the thing represented. Rather it is the beauty of precision, the beauty that becomes evident when nonessentials are stripped away—in other words, the beauty of pure function.[14]

Glaha's image of the dam's transformers, *Portion of 287.5 Kv. Transformers, Roof Take-off Structures* (1938), for example, is similar to Sheeler's photograph *View of Boulder Dam* (1939). Glaha's photograph also resembles another Sheeler picture, *Boulder Dam, Transmission Towers* (1939), which was the basis for Sheeler's 1940 oil painting *Conversation: Sky and Earth*. In addition to the topical similarity of these works, they all distill the scene down to a few summary elements: the relationship between the towering steel and metal and the uncluttered sky above. Further, in each instance the medium utilized is subordinated to the desired effect; minimal brush strokes and photographic manipulation place the focus on the subject matter. The images, with their low-level perspective, are reminiscent of similar studies of the time, such as Rodchenko's pine trees in Pushkino Park.

Portion of 287.5 Kv. Transformers, Roof Take-off Structures for Units N-1 to N-4 Inclusive, from Ramp at Elevation 673.0. April 12, 1938.

View of Boulder Dam. Charles Sheeler. 1939.

Boulder Dam, Transmission Towers. Charles Sheeler. 1939.

Conversation: Sky and Earth. Charles Sheeler. 1940. Oil on canvas.

Glaha's construction images also share commonalities with Sheeler's photographs of the Ford Motor Company's River Rouge plant. For example, Sheeler's *Ingot Molds, Open Hearth Building—Ford Plant* (1927) is strikingly similar to Glaha's *Interior of the Boulder Canyon Project Plant of the Babcock and Wilcox Company* (before 1935). Both photographs share a slightly off-center vantage point and above-ground-level point of view. Also, the clerestory windows in both photographs are framed so that they form lines receding into the background. The windows' converging lines are in turn repeated by similarly diminishing structural forms on the plant floors. Finally, there is yet another commonality between the two men's methodologies. When Sheeler photographed Ford's manufacturing complex, he selected thirty-two photographs that he published independently as artworks.[15] Glaha, too, culled his photographs to create a portfolio of images that was the basis for a series of art exhibitions. Glaha's portfolio photographs, and the exhibitions in which they appeared, will be discussed later.

Margaret Bourke-White's work for *Fortune* magazine contributed to the overall development of machine iconography and specifically influenced Glaha technically and thematically. By the time *Fortune* appeared in 1930, Bourke-White had established herself as a photographer who could address virtually any modern topic, from a city skyline to the Otis Steel Company. The latter topic was particularly challenging technically, in that she sought to capture the flow of molten slag while balancing the high contrast between the darkened factory and the brilliant liquid metal. When they met in 1935, Bourke-White and Glaha likely compared notes on the technical challenges of photographing in low-light situations, she in the steel factory and he in the tunnels at Hoover Dam.

Bourke-White's work was exactly what *Fortune*'s founder, Henry Luce, sought to fulfill his dream of "giving business its own literature, as history and politics had theirs."[16] Luce's goal was not simply the documentation of industry; instead, he wished to imbue it with the poetic allusions of Bourke-White's interpretive style. The result was that, even in the Swift and Company meatpacking plant, she was able to find the formal beauty of repeated lines in pig carcasses strung up on a conveyer belt. Bourke-White, as Vicki Goldberg put it, "gave the country technology as Americans wished to see it. Factories in her pictures were invested with the drama of light, of monumental power, of startling views: industry as theatre."[17] If the Bureau of Reclamation had an unwritten policy regarding how it would ideally like images of Hoover Dam to appear to the public, the preceding statement might well have summarized it beautifully. The stylistic precedents Bourke-White set in *Fortune* in the early 1930s helped Glaha to conduct his own project. Both artists had a flair not only for presenting the practical, functional side of industry but also for finding in it formal beauty and the opportunity for personal interpretation.

Lewis Hine also created photographs based on his personal interpretation of American industry. However, whereas Glaha, Sheeler, and Bourke-White did not specifically examine the role of the worker in relation to the increasing mechanization of America, Hine made the worker-machine rela-tionship the focal point of many of his images from the 1920s into the 1930s. While Glaha, Sheeler, and Bourke-White dedicated themselves to interpreting the hierarchy and physical ramifications of machinery on the urban landscape, Hine sought to determine the role of the workers who operated and maintained those machines.[18] Alan Trachtenberg states, "The aim was to show not industry in a posi-tive light but the worker."[19] In his "work portraits" of men in industry of the 1920s and 1930s, Hine strove to reveal the personal aspect of the worker as he labored, expecting that the work portraits "would help a worker see the beauty and greatness of his work." Unfortunately, Hine's work did not appeal to the public. With the onset of increased mechanization, previous public sentiment for craftsmen had been redirected toward simplified industrial totems: lines, angles, shapes, and steam.[20] But even with the addition of the human element, Hine's photographs retain a static, staged feeling. There is tension in his images created by the juxtaposition of men and their machines, but a true sense of dramatic conflict is missing.[21] Glaha's photographs are also devoid of conflict, although for an entirely different reason. To imply or to photographically depict worker strife or friction would have contravened the image of working conditions at the site that the Bureau wished to portray. To Glaha and the Bureau, the dam's very existence belied the fact that it was built by Depression-era workers. Its higher function was its representational image as a modern mechanistic structure designed to pave the way for a better life by providing water to an arid countryside.[22]

Hine's goal was to celebrate rather than to virtually eliminate the worker, and in that sense he diverged thematically from Glaha, Sheeler, and Bourke-White. Yet because Hine's workers were de-picted in conjunction with their respective machines, he could not help but address those mechanisms as well. Hine's Empire State Building series, for example, while ostensibly about the workers, conveys a great deal about the physical structure, from the way it was constructed to its inherent play of inter-secting lines and planes. Like Glaha, Hine had tackled the photographic documentation of a construc-tion project on an unprecedented scale. A Hine image from the Empire State Building series, *Empire State Building, New York City* (1930/1931), and Glaha's Hoover Dam photograph *Riggers on Boom of Twelve-Ton Crane at Nevada Intake Towers* (1933) (see p. 51) bear witness to the striking similarity between the two men's efforts. Both photographs show figures scaling construction cranes. In keeping with the prevailing aesthetic of the period, neither image provides any reference to the ground on which the cranes are positioned; the geometry of each machine is isolated against the sky. Human forms emerge as if playing within the angles and spaces created by the steel and wires. Both images offer information about the job being performed, but the action is couched within a carefully com-posed intersection of parallel and converging lines.

At this juncture it is important to mention the broader artistic context of the Machine Aes-

Ingot Molds, Open Hearth Building—Ford Plant. Charles Sheeler. 1927.

Interior of the Boulder Canyon Project Plant of the Babcock and Wilcox Company. Before 1935.

Empire State Building, New York City. Lewis W. Hine. 1930/1931.

thetic. The topic was explored by American artists working in nonphotographic media as well. The significance of nonphotographic works of art is twofold. First, Glaha looked for inspiration and affirmation from artists, like Charles Sheeler, who presented some of their most prominent industrial images as oil paintings.[23] Since Glaha was well-rounded culturally and therefore certainly aware of contemporary art trends, he was likely influenced not only by photographers but by artists working in other media as well.[24] Second, the philosophical ideals espoused by some artists, particularly the individuals who sought to promote America's industrial and technical leadership, were congruent with those shared by Glaha and Bureau administrators. While it was not specifically recorded that Bureau officials were influenced by contemporary art trends, photographic or otherwise, it is known that, like Glaha, Bureau managers were generally cultivated and well-read individuals who would understand why machine imagery was a prevalent form of artistic expression. Examples of Machine Aesthetic art were accessible, for instance, through Bourke-White's work in *Fortune* magazine, art exhibitions, and other forums.

Glaha employed all aspects of his artistic knowledge to record and interpret technology. His Machine Aesthetic awareness is reflected in his Hoover Dam photographs, including *Detail of Roof Slab and Beam Reinforcement in Canyon Wall Valve-House Structure*. Certainly the image responded to its primary function of providing a clear visual record of how, specifically, the structural reinforcement was accomplished. However, instead of simply standing perpendicular to the receding lines of the steel reinforcements, Glaha places his camera at a slight angle, thereby creating visual interest in the image because the vertical lines of the composition begin to converge in the upper right-hand corner of the photograph. Further, he has placed his hat, ostensibly for scale, in the middle of the left-hand side of the image; its circular shape serves as a geometric juxtaposition to the convergence of straight lines in the upper right-hand corner. Glaha also elected to frame the image without reference to the larger context within which the reinforcement is situated. Such physically close examinations of engineering subjects are quite typical of the "new aesthetic." Without the title providing specific descriptive information, it would be reasonable to interpret the image as a formalist abstract composition.

In the picture *Workmen Ascending Downstream Face of Dam on Skip Operating over Skids*, Glaha employs the newfound method of shooting at a sharp downward angle at the men rather than placing himself on their level. He precisely composed the image by releasing the shutter at the moment when the workers are centered within the picture plane. As a result, a vertical line descending from the upper left-hand corner to the lower right-hand corner serves to bisect the picture, with the skip situated directly at the midpoint of this descending line. Here again, Glaha is literally using a new perspective at the construction site, and in so doing he is providing visually interesting compositions.

In yet a third example, *Four-Cubic-Yard-Capacity Transit Mixer Discharging Concrete*, Glaha depicts how a four-cubic-yard mixer is employed to discharge cement in areas too confined to permit entry of the eight-cubic-yard mixers. He incorporates a viewpoint in which the subject of the photograph is carefully framed by a nearly symmetrical array of lines and angles. Here the artistic emphasis is not on an unusual camera angle but on the way in which a pleasing visual composition can be found in an industrial setting.

Changes in photographic methods were complemented by photographers who narrowed their focus of attention to specific categories. At the turn of the century, Eugene Atget explored the environs of a changing and often enervated Paris, and in 1910 August Sander began focusing on individuals and groups he found to be representative of various professions and classes in Germany. Sheeler, as mentioned, documented the Ford Motor Company's manufacturing plant in Michigan, and in 1929 he likewise concentrated on Chartres Cathedral. Perhaps most closely related to Glaha's work is Lewis Hine's 1930–31 series of Empire State Building construction photographs.

Glaha's Bureau photographs were, obviously, limited to a specific topic. Further, in 1934 Commissioner Mead instructed Glaha to create "a special volume of photographs of operations on the Boulder Canyon project."[25] As a result, Glaha designed and created portfolios containing forty-four of his photographs tipped in. Each photograph was hand-titled and was accompanied by a small ink sketch executed by Glaha. The folios, compilations of Glaha's drafting and artistic skills, presumably were meant as presentation pieces for high-ranking officials. In a volume prepared for Interior Secretary Harold Ickes, the handwritten title page states: "Boulder Dam: A Portfolio of Photographs prepared for Hon. Harold L. Ickes, Secretary of the Interior." Below is a sketch of a hard hat resting against a jackhammer, and beneath the sketch is written, "Photographs and Format by B. D. Glaha—Made at Boulder City, Nevada—August 1934 to December 1934."[26] Ickes's folio was most likely meant to be displayed in his office.

Glaha devoted quite a bit of attention to creating this album, and it represents the best and aesthetically most effective photographs from his body of work taken at the dam. The folio opens with *Workman with Water Bag*, an image of a bare-chested workman, his head thrown back, drinking from a water bag. That particular image functions as something of an icon for the entire project. The singular man, captured with no tools in his hand, symbolizes the many individuals who tamed the Colorado River with brawn and intellect. The water bag alludes to the river, to the very focus of the man's efforts. Bringing drinking water to a single person, which in turn fuels him to complete the monumental task at hand, refers to the Bureau's effort to direct water for drinking and irrigation to millions of people.

The next image, *Nevada Desert Landscape near Boulder City*, is a shot of the dry, barren, and inhospitable setting for the Bureau's efforts. To highlight the dramatic change that water could make on arid land, Glaha follows the desert photograph with a series of images depicting Boulder City. He

Workman with Water Bag. Before 1935.

Nevada Desert Landscape near Boulder City. Before 1935.

emphasizes the verdure of the town versus the aridity of the desert by showing Boulder City not in its initial phase of development but after trees, lawns, and flower beds were introduced, as in *Street Scene in Residential Section, Boulder City.*

From his images of Boulder City, Glaha shifts attention to the construction of the dam. Beginning with *Black Canyon Prior to Boulder Dam Construction,* Glaha then depicts the drilling and blasting of the canyon walls in preparation for the concrete in *Blasting in Boulder Dam Abutment Excavations.* Certain specific tasks, such as placing the concrete lining in the diversion tunnel bores and welding the thirty-foot penstocks, are then pictured, as well as the exterior and interior of the Babcock and Wilcox Company steel-forming plant. Interspersed throughout these images are chronologically ordered shots of the dam rising from the floor of Black Canyon, as in *The Downstream Face of Boulder Dam as Seen from Lookout Point*; examples of specific construction techniques, such as *Steel Bar Reinforcement in Boulder Dam Intake Towers*; and the dam's appurtenant works, as in *One of the Two Spillway Structures at Boulder Dam.* Following these construction images is a photograph showing a power transmission line. The transmission line symbolizes that one of the main purposes of the dam, the generation of electrical power, benefits Americans living far from Black Canyon. The final image is that of the dam at night, *The Upstream Face of Boulder Dam during the Night Shift.*

What significance do the portfolio's images have compared with the thousands of other photographs Glaha produced during the construction of Boulder Dam and Boulder City? Can it be said that some or all of these images were created with the intent of presenting them in something other than primarily utilitarian venues? Glaha once stated that regardless of their purpose, he always strove to create images that were "attractive as well as technically sound as it is possible to make."[27] He meant that even in situations where his photographs were meant only to illustrate, for example, a technical government report, he tried to produce the best images he could in terms of their composition and print quality. However, the argument can be made that, at times, Glaha specifically sought to create photographs in which any utilitarian component was secondary to formal or iconographic intentions. Four images from the folio can be singled out to highlight Glaha's aim and ability to produce images that go beyond documentation by incorporating iconographic, heroic, or formal aspects, thereby creating "symbol" pictures meant to convey ideological concepts rather than facts or information.

The first of these images, *Workman with Water Bag,* clearly was composed with the iconographic components mentioned above in mind. The workman stands on a jumble of sharp rocks, surrounded by piping and other construction equipment; the water bag obscures his face, thereby rendering him anonymous. His anonymity endows him with an Everyman status, enabling him to symbolize all the workers on the job site. His singularity is further enhanced by Glaha's use of a short focal length, which causes the other workers in the background to appear out of focus. Finally, Glaha

Street Scene in Residential Section, Boulder City. Before 1935.

Blasting in Boulder Dam Abutment Excavations. Before 1935.

The Downstream Face of Boulder Dam as Seen from Lookout Point. Before 1935.

Steel Bar Reinforcement in Boulder Dam Intake Towers. Before 1935.

One of the Two Spillway Structures at Boulder Dam. Before 1935.

The Upstream Face of Boulder Dam during the Night Shift. Before 1935.

successfully conveys the workman's heroic quality. His bare, muscled flesh works in defiance of the parched, craggy canyon. The contrasting elements of man and nature imbue the image with a visual power that transcends more casual photographs of workers *in situ*.

Rigger on Cableway Headtower during Construction conveys a sense of heroism. The photograph shows a worker standing at the pinnacle of the tower, feet firmly planted on the steel supports so that he appears to be integrated into the structure. The man is small in proportion to the headtower, river, and canyon walls around him, yet his stance conveys a sense of power and mastery of the situation. The "human" element, the flesh and muscle of the man, are again in contrast to the surrounding steel, rock, and water. Above all, there is the sense that man is in control of both nature and his constructs.

However, Glaha did not need to incorporate human elements into his images in order to imbue his photographs with aesthetic qualities. His *Interior of Construction Cableway Headtower* is an excellent example of his ability to celebrate the repetition of shapes and contrasting textures of the functional machinery. By cropping the overall scene, Glaha intentionally limits the visual information, thereby placing emphasis on the cylindrical shapes of the cable spools and the rectilinearity of the corrugated tower walls. The repeated lines of the wound cable echo the wall corrugations and are in contrast to the angled steel beam supports. The human figures and rough, irregularly textured canyon walls, so dominant in the two previous images, are now relegated to minor supporting elements. The photograph clearly evidences Glaha's awareness of the Machine Aesthetic.

Finally, *Boulder Dam Spillway Drum Gates and Piers* presents the formal geometry of the dam's concrete and steel elements without any visual reference to the canyon or river. Appropriately, the image is at the end of the folio because the photograph conveys the completion of the dam as a building project. The picture also heralds the end of the construction site's chaotic movement of tailings, building materials, vehicular traffic, and workmen. The pure beauty and size of the spillway alone remain to be studied. The photograph epitomizes the fact that a man-made construct has been placed where a river once freely flowed. The photographer's perspective, from the bottom of the spillway, monumentalizes the size of the spillway walls, drum gates, and piers versus the size of the figures seated atop the drum gate. Glaha has cropped the image, thereby reducing its informational aspect and increasing its inherent abstraction.

Given the exceptional aesthetic quality of Glaha's portfolio photographs, it is likely that these were the images he utilized for a series of exhibitions he had beginning in January 1935.[28] The western landscape painter Maynard Dixon was the catalyst for Glaha's January–February 1935 exhibition at the DeYoung Museum of Art in San Francisco.[29] Dixon had been to the dam site, where he completed canvases under the Public Works of Art Project, and subsequently became acquainted with Glaha and

Rigger on Cableway Headtower during Construction. Before 1935.

Interior of Construction Cableway Headtower. Before 1935.

Boulder Dam Spillway Drum Gates and Piers. Before 1935.

his photographic work. Dixon was so impressed with Glaha's work that he took a group of his images and showed them to the DeYoung Museum's Exhibits Committee. The response of the committee, relayed in a letter from Dixon to Glaha, was as follows:

> I took the liberty of showing your prints to the people at the DeYoung Museum who were very much impressed and immediately mentioned the possibility of a showing. . . . The Museum has a good discriminating audience, good professional comment and lots of the people interested in Boulder Dam. I want you and your work to get the benefits of a show—a *good* show here, and I believe the DeYoung is the right place.[30]

The exhibition was well received; some 250,000 people viewed the fifty prints on display, and Glaha's work was the subject of a lecture by renowned photographer and critic Ansel Adams.[31] Clearly, Glaha's images were being presented in a different context; instead of serving a more overtly political purpose for the Bureau, they were being displayed within the context of art photography. Walker Young argued in favor of the exhibition on the basis that it would "reach a very discriminating audience and would be the means of the project, and indirectly the entire Public Works program, receiving a great deal of very favorable and dignified publicity."[32]

From the DeYoung, the images traveled to the Fine Arts Gallery in San Diego, California, where they were on display during March 1935. In the local paper, the gallery's curator, Julia Gethman Andrews, wrote of Glaha's pictures, "The photographs are exciting, in subject matter and in pattern, some of them are as fine as any that Alfred Stieglitz has exhibited in his portrayal of the machine age. . . . [T]here are aesthetic elements in Ben Glaha's work which reap the results of outstanding men in this field, such as Clarence White."[33] Andrews's praise validates Glaha's ability to function as a fine-art photographer.

From the Fine Arts Gallery, the images traveled to the Haggin Museum in Stockton, California, for exhibition from April 28 to May 25, 1935.[34] Commentary on the Stockton exhibition again celebrated the artistic aspects of the images of the dam's construction. Museum Director Harry Noyes Pratt commented: "Whether one is an enthusiastic amateur photographer or is merely interested in Boulder Dam as one of the wonders of the modern world, this group of 50 photographs by Ben Glaha is worth making an effort to see. It is obvious to the artist-photographer that Glaha has taken infinite delight in the pattern and design."[35] While the director remarked on the formal aspects of the images, another reviewer focused on the fact that the images struck a balance between recording actual construction scenes and providing more aesthetic components: "We hadn't thought of a man putting a bolt in a steel crosspiece as material for an artist until we saw the photographs of Boulder Dam taken by Ben

Glaha for the United States Reclamation Board. Now we realize what can be done by the man who knows how."[36]

In May 1935, Construction Engineer Young requested from Commissioner Mead permission for Glaha to produce "exhibition" or "salon" prints. Young's request was a consequence of the exposure Glaha's work received in the art galleries and the resultant increase in public demand for the sale of his carefully printed and signed photographs. By creating images classified as "exhibition" prints, Young argued to the commissioner, those images could be sold for a higher price than "ordinary commercial work."[37] Young based his argument on his belief that "the value of prints of this nature lies in the fact that they are the work of an individual and bear the signature of the artist, in keeping with the authenticity demanded."[38] Commissioner Mead readily approved the plan to sell "exhibition" prints upon order. He couched his approval in terms supportive of the images' aesthetic possibilities: "I do not wish to be greedy, but I hope you will see that the office is furnished copies of material prepared for exhibition. They are excellent 'scenery' for the office and give us a welcome feeling of having something unusually fine to offer when requests are made for exhibition purposes."[39]

No documentation exists regarding whether the Bureau achieved any significant income gain as a result of the sale of the prints. However, the Bureau did gain public exposure as a result of the photographs' sale and exhibition.

In an effort to broaden political support on the east coast, in August 1935, Glaha's images were displayed at the National Museum.[40] Letters from Commissioner Mead, announcing the exhibition of photographs "by Ben Glaha, official photographer of the Bureau of Reclamation at Boulder Dam," indicated that the images were placed "in the building which houses the Lindbergh plane." Copies of the letter were sent to such government figures as House of Representatives members from fifteen western states and the president's cabinet. The recipients of the letters, as well as their friends and associated personnel, were encouraged to view the photographs.[41] In one version of the letter, Commissioner Mead stated: "I hope you will find an opportunity to visit the gallery and see how admirably the medium of construction activity has lent itself to faithful and artistic recording by camera."[42]

The key terms in the commissioner's statement are "faithful" and "artistic," another way of stating the 1930s documentary trend of combining reality and emotion in documentaries. He emphasizes the "faithful" aspect of the images to promote them as veridical documents that accurately convey the construction process. By also acknowledging the images' "artistic" aspects, he compliments Glaha's eye for selecting and presenting images that are visually pleasing as well. The photographs' aura of factuality functioned in concert with the Bureau's propagandistic use of the photographs to publicize the necessity and efficiency of the project. The fact that the images were so visually appealing further facilitated their sale and promotion.[43]

Ben Glaha could have simply produced accurate and somewhat visually appealing photographs of Hoover Dam's construction. However, he was not inclined to produce what he would have considered average photographs. Instead, he challenged himself to explore new techniques and thereby contributed to the advancement not only of documentary photography but of creative methodologies in fine-art photography as well. The Bureau of Reclamation was adroit enough to encourage Glaha's inclinations. As a result, the photographs Glaha produced not only fulfilled the Bureau's documentary requirements but also opened up the entirely new promotional venues of museum exhibitions and photographic print sales.

5
DOCUMENTS FOR PUBLICITY
The Photographs as Propaganda

The Bureau of Reclamation's success in using photographs to promote its Hoover Dam construction project can be attributed to the dichotomous nature of Glaha's photographs; their aesthetic beauty enticed viewer interest while their documentary style served the Bureau's propagandistic intentions. Because Hoover Dam was erected in the 1930s, there were no televised news programs to visually convey the construction developments to the American public. The government therefore vigorously utilized visually appealing still photographs, carefully released to a variety of print media, to place the government-funded project in the best possible light.[1] While some motion picture documentation was made of the construction process (including Bureau movies shot by Glaha), still images were more easily controlled and distributed, and therefore became the federal government's primary publicity vehicle.

The topic of this chapter is the array of print media in which Ben Glaha's photographs appeared in order to meet the Bureau's expansive propagandistic needs. In each instance, Bureau-approved images were presented in a truthful and enticing manner for the purpose of promoting the project. In a letter to the Commissioner of the Bureau of Reclamation, Elwood Mead, Chief Engineer R. F. Walter stated, "Nothing the Bureau sends out is exaggerated, but Government reports can be colored to make them more readable."[2] The Bureau's doctoring of information was hardly a novel approach, but what set its efforts apart from those of other agencies was its prolific use of photographs to substantiate the project's efficacy.

At the project's beginning, Bureau officials realized that to best promote its public policies most effectively, it would need to exert control over the content and distribution of the construction images. For example, before Glaha began photographing Hoover Dam there was some internal debate as to whether a Bureau photographer or an outside contractor should be hired. Construction Engineer Walker Young suggested that by "granting an exclusive concession to some outside firm," a "satisfactory photographic record" could be obtained, "but this seems very doubtful for the reason that their requirements and ours would not be the same."[3] Young did not spell out what, specifically, would differentiate the Bureau's requirements from those of another individual or organization. He was likely referring to the Bureau's need for a broad range of images, as exemplified by the Glaha photographs examined in Chapter 3, as well as specific images that favorably portrayed the Bureau in such areas as project safety and the fair treatment of workers.

Because the Bureau worked intimately with Six Companies, one option was to utilize photographs taken by the Six Companies photographer, Walter J. Lubken. That option, however, was rejected. The admitted reason for functioning independently of Six Companies was the competition between the two organizations. The Bureau was concerned that if too much publicity went to Six Companies, "the public will not know that we have anything to do with the Boulder Canyon Project. . . . [T]he Bureau is bound to be overshadowed by Six Companies, Inc."[4] What the Bureau may not have been willing to state openly was its concern over the frank manner in which Six Companies recorded the difficult and dangerous conditions on the project site. Six Companies did not hesitate to publish images that graphically portrayed the extremely hot temperatures and physical dangers the workers confronted. Photographs depicting unsafe working conditions contradicted the unwritten Bureau policy prohibiting publicity that reported hazardous conditions at the construction site.[5]

The Bureau therefore began to produce and release its own selected images and text. In those instances where the Bureau released materials to outside organizations, it sought to regulate how that information was utilized, as specified in Order No. 630, dated May 20, 1933, from Secretary of the Interior Harold Ickes: "No publicity matter with reference to the Department, or with reference to any individual in the Department in his official capacity, is to be given without the approval of the Executive Assistant in Charge of Publicity, or of the Secretary."[6] Most outside agencies and individuals offered the Bureau a draft text for review prior to publication, and the Bureau did not hesitate to edit the work to meet its specifications.[7]

Washington could not receive updated images from the dam site quickly enough to satisfy the public's interest in the project. In April 1932, Acting Commissioner M. A. Schnurr wrote to Walker Young, "We are constantly being called upon for photographs of the work at the dam site."[8] As a result of such popular demand, Bureau photographs (the majority of which were taken by Glaha) and Bureau-approved texts appeared in newspapers, magazines, pamphlets, books, and slides.

The daily newspapers were the easiest and fastest way to report the construction's progress. Furthermore, because newspapers are usually quick to place spectacular pictures on their front pages to promote circulation, photographs of the dam's construction were a welcome addition to national and foreign papers. Initially, Commissioner Mead requested that all publicity information be released to the large press associations through the Bureau's Washington office despite Construction Engineer Young's desire to deal directly with the local papers.[9] Commissioner Mead stated his wish that Young "realize the importance of utilizing the large press associations to the best advantage and at the same time protect[ing] the Bureau from unfavorable publicity."[10] A compromise was later struck when the Washington office of the Associated Press requested that from time to time Glaha's photographs be made available to its Los Angeles Bureau. Commissioner Mead approved the arrangement provided that the written releases continued to be issued from Washington.[11]

It is worth noting that at this point in the development of institutional advertising, the differentiation between "public" and "press" relations was just beginning to emerge.[12] Dedicated internal departments or contract companies hired to handle public relations issues were rare. More typically, information was "leaked" to the press, which was responsible for its distribution.

Two dramatic examples of images the Bureau released to newspapers for the specific purpose of validating and publicizing its efforts are Glaha's *Upstream Face of Boulder Dam during the Night Shift* and *High Scalers Drilling into Canyon Wall 500 Feet above the Colorado River in Black Canyon.* The night scene appeared in the *New York Times* and the *Washington Star.*[13] The utilization of the night image is symbolic of the ability of Glaha's images to function on two different levels: the photograph's eye-catching chiaroscuro attracted readers, and at the same time the image conveyed information about the dramatic scale and potential power of the nearly completed dam. The underlying political message was that work on the dam was diligently being conducted night and day to expedite completion of a critically needed water management project. The photograph of the drillers is also visually arresting. Glaha carefully framed the image so that the two drill power cables in the central foreground lead the viewer's eye to the two workmen precariously positioned on the edge of the cliff. However, upon closer examination, it is apparent that each man is tethered to the rock wall by a safety line. The newspaper caption for the photograph expressed exaggerated, even hubristic, confidence in the project. It reads, "Public Works—'The Program Reaches Proportions Which Make Such Enterprises as the Building of the Pyramids Seem Almost Petty.'"[14]

The magazines in which Glaha's photographs appeared were quite varied in their content, yet his images were adaptable to the nature of each publication and always promoted the Bureau's efforts at Hoover Dam. The majority of magazines utilizing his photographs were technically oriented. For example, the Bureau's in-house publication *Reclamation Era* celebrated the progress of its irrigation projects and their resultant agricultural benefits. Two instances of the use of Glaha's images in *Reclamation Era* are a one-page spread of captioned photographs covering the Boulder Canyon Project and a general article about the development of Boulder City.[15] His more eye-catching images were sometimes placed on the front or back cover of the magazine, such as his *Upstream Face of Boulder Dam during the Night Shift.*[16] The visually arresting night scene was selected as cover art because of its advertising potential. *Reclamation Era* was, of course, circulated among Bureau employees, but it was

High Scalers Drilling into Canyon Wall 500 Feet above the Colorado River in Black Canyon. August 1, 1932.

also used for publicity purposes. For example, when Rotary Club International requested information about the dam to give to a Peruvian member who was planning to visit there, Acting Commissioner Dent sent several copies of *Reclamation Era*. The issues contained "articles in regard to the progress of construction work at Boulder Dam and the present status of the project."[17]

Another excellent example of the utilization of Glaha's photographs occurred in conjunction with the trade magazine *Electrical West*. In October 1936, *Electrical West* produced the publication *Boulder Dam Power: A Pictorial History*, the stated purpose of which was "a permanent record of construction technique and engineering design employed from dam site to completion."[18] The Glaha images incorporated were of a bottom-dump, eight-cubic-yard cement bucket, a view of the piping for the cooling system, a finished penstock section placed within the tunnel, and the centralized control panels for all the equipment in the powerhouse. The photographs are carefully arranged in concert with other images to form a pleasing visual overview of the construction progress and techniques. Information regarding the scale, location, and arrangement of the various components of the dam is pictorially conveyed. Through the photographs' exposure to a large technical and interested lay readership, the Bureau and the project both gained positive recognition.

In addition to technically oriented magazines, Glaha's photographs appeared in art magazines. The inclusion of Glaha's images in both technical and art publications reiterates two important hallmarks of his photographs: the dichotomy of the images' documentary style and artistic merit, and the Bureau's sanctioning of Glaha's artistic efforts as a means of generating recognition for the project. On the occasion of Glaha's receipt of the Department of the Interior's Distinguished Service Award, the Bureau commended both components of his imagery:

> His photographs have been used and published widely not only for their functional purposes but also as works of artistic quality. Recognition of his work has reflected credit on him as well as the Bureau of Reclamation. He has consistently avoided the temptation to measure his accomplishments exclusively by artistic standards, but has, by his ability, achieved remarkably high standards of both functional and artistic results.[19]

The high artistic quality of Glaha's photographs qualified his work to appear in art-oriented publications such as *Camera Craft* and *U.S. Camera*. In the April 1935 issue of *Camera Craft*, a selection of his Hoover Dam photographs accompanied an article on his work by the art photographer Willard Van Dyke. Van Dyke stated that "Glaha's significance as an artist and a photographer lies in the fact that he has not turned his back on the subject material offered him in his regular line of duty. For the first time, to my knowledge, a man who is hired to do a big recording job, also turns out photographs of rare beauty from every standpoint."[20] One of the photographs utilized in the article, *Grouting Con-*

crete Lining in Fifty-Foot-Diameter Diversion Tunnel, had also been published in more technically oriented publications, such as *Reclamation Era* and the Bureau's 1932 *Annual Project History*.[21] Within the context of the *Camera Craft* essay, the image is celebrated for its aesthetic qualities as well; the scale and specifics of a construction procedure are conveyed in concert with Glaha's creative use of framing and chiaroscuro.[22]

Similarly, in an article Glaha wrote for the January–February 1939 issue of *U.S. Camera*, his straightforward and precise Hoover Dam photographs illustrated formal compositional qualities. Regarding his imagery, he stated, "After all, its [a photograph's] purpose is to illustrate or to analyze; and it has gone a long way toward meeting this requirement if it is visually lucid and pleasing."[23] One of the photographs included in the *U.S. Camera* article is his *Arizona Intake Towers as Seen from Surface of Reservoir*. The repeating vertical lines of the towers and near-vertical shadow on the upstream dam face are juxtaposed against the dam's horizontal concrete seams and the canyon wall's crest. The smoothness of the man-made concrete structures stands in contrast to the ruggedness of the canyon walls. The image supplies information about the dam's structure and at the same time monumentalizes it. The photograph explains the placement of the towers on two rock ledges near the canyon wall, and the low camera angle exaggerates the size of the towers so that they appear to dominate the canyon wall and dam face. Because the Bureau sanctioned the broad use of Glaha's photographs in publications such as *Camera Craft* and *U.S. Camera*, the readers of those periodicals—a large body of professional photographers and art enthusiasts—became more familiar with the Bureau's project.

Newspapers and magazines, however, were not the only places in which the Bureau sanctioned placement of Glaha's photographs. Numerous pamphlets and booklets, addressing a variety of topics, utilized his photographs. Two publications by independent companies incorporating Bureau-issued photographs are *View-Book of the Boulder Dam* and *Boulder Dam: A Modern Engineering Triumph*.[24]

The *View-Book*, intended as a souvenir, combined photographs and drawings to provide a pictorial overview of the construction process. Among the photographs in the book was Glaha's well-publicized night view of the dam. A portion of the propagandistic caption accompanying the night shift image reads, "Construction proceeds during three 8-hour shifts each day seven days a week." By including the photograph, the booklet acquires a dramatic image while the Bureau's dedication to rapid completion of the project is reiterated.

The publication of *Boulder Dam: A Modern Engineering Triumph* by the Barrett Company was clearly self-serving, while at the same time it promoted the Bureau's efforts. The Barrett Company provided materials for the construction of the powerhouse roof and the enamel used to waterproof the thirty-five-foot-diameter steel penstocks and connecting penstocks.[25] By proclaiming the magnitude

Grouting Concrete Lining in Fifty-Foot-Diameter Diversion Tunnel. Before 1935.

Arizona Intake Towers as Seen from Surface of Reservoir. The water surface is at an elevation of 884 feet, and the base of the intake towers is at an elevation of 895 feet. June 21, 1935.

and technical challenges of the task, along with advertising the company's specific contribution to the project's successful completion, both parties received publicity.[26] Glaha's photograph of a section of pipe being lowered into the canyon, *Handling Thirty-Foot-Diameter Steel Penstock Pipe by Cableway*, visually emphasizes the physical size of the project. Companion text such as the following conveyed an underlying emotional context:

> Who is there that even today does not thrill to the stories of the early pioneers of the West — of the covered wagon days — of hardships endured — of battles won — of heroic courage, fortitude and optimism that made possible the settling of vast territories and the development of great natural resources in the nation? Today we have a modern parallel to the conquering of the West in the completion of a remarkable engineering achievement — THE BUILDING OF BOULDER DAM.[27]

In actuality, the Barrett Company's contribution to the dam's completion was limited because the products it supplied were peripheral and pertained to areas secondary to the overall project. By producing a booklet with a dozen pages of photographs and text, the entire effort and the Barrett Company's contribution were highlighted, and the Bureau was only too happy to accept recognition as the overseer of such an endeavor.[28]

It is worth mentioning that, as overblown as the Barrett Company's text seems today, in the 1930s such dramatic rhetoric was frequently used to convey a corporate agenda. Favored terms of the time included "story," "adventure," and "spectacle" — for example, *The Story of Hoover Dam*. While the use of such words may seem a quaint way of rendering a complex issue readable and congenial, it actually had a very specific public relations function. Ulrich Keller addressed the issue when he stated: "Since the 1930s, American industry was indeed determined, not to give accurate information to the public, but rather 'to tell its story,' and the respected handbook *Publicity in Action* succinctly stated that 'publicity' is the technique of 'telling the story' of any organization, person or cause."[29] Those stories were, of course, the recounting of events from one author's (corporate or individual) point of view. That point of view was unfailingly in favor of the business's or government's actions.

Keller relates how one private business successfully employed the story concept in its publicity by citing Roy Stryker's documentation project to enhance the poor public image of Standard Oil of New Jersey. The public's perception of Standard Oil's ethics was damaged by allegations that it collaborated with a German oil company prior to World War II. Stryker employed the story concept and "remained conscious of the fact that even a sociologically founded method of *telling* the oil *story* meant, in the final analysis, the *selling* of the oil *ideology*."[30] To that end, Stryker commissioned, then released as propaganda, thousands of photographs of the oil and automobile corporations. With those images, he sold the American public a vision of itself as a literally mobile nation in which democratic pluralism and other American values were readily accessible along the highways and byways of the nation. The Bureau was likewise attempting to sell an ideology, one rooted in the benefits of water resource management. What better way to accomplish this goal than by pairing images with carefully chosen text that, together, would guide the reader's perception?

Other essential elements in the Bureau's propagandistic efforts regarding the dam were booklets and pamphlets about the dam created for distribution to the general public. Whether handed out at the dam site or disseminated as an enticement to visit the dam, the publications were carefully balanced to be didactic yet visceral. Some of the publications were multipage volumes covering the entire construction of the dam, such as *Construction of Boulder Dam*. This book chronologically traces the rise of the dam while highlighting various components of the structure, such as its location, cableways, concrete mixing plant, diversion tunnels, intake towers, building materials, outlet works, personnel, spillways, and tunnels. Many of Glaha's eye-catching images were used to illustrate *Construction of Boulder Dam*, for example his *Eight-Cubic-Yard-Capacity Concrete Bucket Discharging Load in Dam Column Form*. The intent of the text and images was to convey to the reader the "story" of the dam's construction process while allowing him/her to vicariously experience each phase of the construction program.[31]

Other illustrated Bureau publications were in single-sheet foldout leaflet form, "prepared as an educational souvenir to be distributed to the children who see our Boulder Dam films in their schools . . . for distribution to casual visitors at the project headquarters and for distribution with requests for general information."[32] In each instance, photographs and text were carefully combined for specific purposes. For example, the versions produced during and approaching the end of the construction process focused most heavily on the building program. In a Bureau of Reclamation leaflet titled *Boulder Dam* (ca. 1936) Glaha photographs, such as *Downstream Face of Dam Showing Powerhouse Footings*, were included to explain construction techniques while also alluding to the rapid rise of the dam and its appurtenant works.[33]

Subsequent leaflets, made immediately prior to, or after, the end of construction, described not only the dam but the surrounding area as well. The leaflet *Boulder Dam: The World's Most Impressive Engineering Spectacle in the Center of an Area of Unsurpassed Scenic and Historical Interest* (undated; ca. 1936?) emphasized that a visit to the dam should incorporate a wide variety of sites and activities—from touring the Grand Canyon or Zion National Park, to water sports on Lake Mead.[34] Glaha's *Map of the Boulder Dam Area Showing the Principal Points of Scenic and Historical Interest* graphically located the many attractions, and his photographs of tourist destinations, such as a restored pueblo and Atlatl Rock's ancient Indian petroglyphs, both located near St. Thomas, Nevada, were included in the

Downstream Face of Dam Showing Powerhouse Footings. This view looks obliquely upstream toward the Arizona abutment. September 27, 1933.

pamphlet.[35] In this leaflet, the dam is presented as the starting point for trips to many surrounding sites and activities.

The switch in emphasis from the dam alone to the inclusion of surrounding attractions indicates the progressive recognition of the dam's existence. The general public had become more familiar with the dam's presence, and many people had already traveled to the dam site. In 1934 and 1935, 750,000 people visited Hoover Dam and Las Vegas.[36] Visitors were encouraged to return to the area to explore the many natural and man-made attractions. Another purpose of the leaflet was to contradict the reputation of the dam site and the surrounding area as inhospitable desert. A drawing of a thermometer in the brochure indicates that the highest average daytime temperature is ninety-three degrees and occurs in the month of July. June, August, and September show readings in the eighty degree range, and January shows a low of forty-eight degrees. Such seemingly comfortable climate statistics were a blatant public relations effort to downplay the frequent triple-digit summertime thermometer readings.[37] The fact that summertime temperatures could render car door handles untouchable without oven mitts probably made the available water sports seem attractive.

A third Bureau leaflet, *Boulder Dam* (undated; ca. 1939?), addresses the construction program and simultaneously strives to emphasize the benefits derived from the dam, including the plan for recouping construction costs via the sale of hydroelectric power.[38] Once more, Glaha's construction images were used in conjunction with carefully worded text. For example, the leaflet states, "While power is a by-product of the dam, the fact that Boulder Dam has made available much cheap energy is important to the future welfare of the whole Southwest."[39]

As evidenced by the leaflets, the Bureau's agenda changed over time, from initially reassuring the public that construction of the dam was feasible, to promoting the benefits gained through downstream water management and electric power generation. Glaha's photographs, matched with carefully crafted text, promoted the Bureau's ideology.[40]

Glaha's Hoover Dam photographs were also used as book illustrations. Like the pamphlets, leaflets, and other publications in which his images appeared, the books' subjects and themes varied greatly. In addition to regular Bureau publications, such as annual project histories, private authors and organizations incorporated Glaha's dam photographs into their manuscripts. Ralph B. Simmons, for example, compiled a broad range of information pertaining to the dam for his book *Boulder Dam and the Great Southwest*. Simmons stated the purpose of his book thus: "A narrative historical, pictorial, and biographical work containing a complete history of the Boulder Canyon Project, the turbulent Colorado River, Grand Canyon, each of the seven Basin States and compact biographical sketches of personalities prominent in the materialization of the Boulder Canyon Project and in the development of southwestern America."[41] In Simmons's text, Glaha's photographs serve to illustrate the process, techniques, and drama of the construction program.

While Simmons's text generally celebrates the benefits the dam brought to the Southwest, a more recent publication, Joseph E. Stevens's book *Hoover Dam: An American Adventure*, is more critical in its examination of the planning, execution, and results of the structure.[42] Glaha's photographs are incorporated to illustrate Stevens's particular perspective. For example, his *Workman with Water Bag*, from the Ickes portfolio, is removed from any aesthetic context and utilized to convey Stevens's contemporary research findings. Publications prior to Stevens's, those of the Bureau in particular, would have the reader believe that all project workers were well cared for and suffered little despite inherent construction hazards and extreme climatic conditions. In fact, as Stevens reveals, in the earliest phase of construction, men toiling in less accessible or dangerous areas often went without water because the water boys could not or would not take water to them. As a result, workers suffered from heat prostration. The water problem, which was later solved, was exemplified by Stevens through his inclusion of Glaha's photograph. In Stevens's book, Glaha's historic photographs were used in conjunction with a contemporary critical evaluation of the overall project.[43]

The federal government also produced books that addressed the building of the dam. Harold L. Ickes, Secretary of the Interior and Administrator of Public Works, penned a text titled *Back to Work: The Story of PWA*.[44] Because in 1934 the PWA (Public Works Administration) allotted $38 million toward the completion of Hoover Dam, Secretary Ickes discussed the dam in his text. His comments, not surprisingly laudatory, were accompanied by one of Glaha's most famous and, as we have seen, well-publicized images, the night scene of construction at Boulder Dam. The night scene photograph gracefully conveys the implied power and proficiency of the project. The photograph's visual message is in sympathy with Secretary Ickes's written comments; the rising form of the dam validates the PWA expenditure on the Bureau's efforts.

Glaha's photographs of the dam's construction continued to appear in a variety of publications, even well after the dam's completion. In *American Building Art: The Twentieth Century*, a Glaha photograph of Hoover Dam appears alongside images of such other famous structures as the Golden Gate Bridge in San Francisco and the Solomon R. Guggenheim Museum in New York City.[45] The Bureau sanctioned use of its images in books that reflected well on its efforts and continued to promote recognition of its projects.

Bureau of Reclamation photographs that traced and lauded Hoover Dam's construction were further disseminated to the general public by means of prepackaged illustrated lectures and exhibitions. Bureau photographs were used to create lantern slides that were matched to a didactic text on the history and building of the dam. Additionally, Bureau prints and transparencies, often enlarged for display, were circulated at state and international expositions. Glaha shot some four thousand negatives of the dam's construction; they comprised the vast majority of Bureau images of the entire construction process. The preponderance of images made into slides, exhibition enlargements, and transparencies were culled from Glaha's work.[46]

Early in the construction program the Bureau began preparing a lantern slide lecture "dealing with the work already done, the original investigations, the planning and building of the dam, and other preparatory work, including the work done so far on the tunnels."[47] The idea was that the lecture would be updated as construction progressed. The presentation was divided into three parts: the general description and history of the project; the design; and the construction progress. The Denver and Washington Bureau offices both retained copies of the lecture so that "local representatives of the bureau can present the material at local meetings of interested organizations."[48]

Commissioner Mead received many requests to speak about the project, but his time was limited. As a result, he came to rely on the slide presentation to represent the Bureau:

> The demand for lectures on the Boulder Canyon project has increased beyond our expectations and I find it will not be possible to accept all of the invitations. In place of having someone from this office talk to the clubs and associations, which are interested in the Boulder Canyon project or other reclamation activities, we can furnish slides and movies concerning a large number of subjects.[49]

The only costs incurred by schools or clubs desiring to use the slide sets were the fees for shipping the slides to and from the organization. Individual slides and slide sets were also for sale. Information regarding slides available for purchase by interested groups and individuals was sent upon request and was advertised in publications such as the booklet *Construction of Boulder Dam*.[50]

Venues such as expositions and museum displays offered the opportunity for semipermanent public exposure to Bureau photographs. As always, prior to approving the request the Bureau verified that the exhibitions would place the images in a positive context. At the 1932 International Colonial and Overseas Exposition at Paris, for example, the Reclamation Service exhibit included large pictures of Hoover Dam.[51] Likewise, the 1935–1936 California Pacific International Exposition in San Diego included a Bureau of Reclamation display that was highlighted by a transparency showing a Hoover Dam construction scene.[52] At the 1939 Golden Gate International Exposition in San Francisco, a large mural of Hoover Dam was positioned above a diorama illustrating the "conversion of desert lands to productive agricultural lands by irrigation."[53] In each instance, written information was distributed to supplement the visual displays.

Bureau photographs were also the foundation of an exhibition installed at the California State Exposition Building at Exposition Park in Los Angeles. The secretary-manager of the building wrote to Acting Commissioner John Page, requesting "photographs of the different units and the topography" from which a Boulder Dam diorama was to be constructed.[54] The Museum of Science and Industry at Jackson Park in Chicago also offered a Hoover Dam model along with a diorama of photographic and diagrammatic material.[55] A more unusual venue for the display of Bureau photographs of Hoover Dam was six New York City ticket offices of the Baltimore and Ohio Railroad.[56] Finally, for interested viewers who were unable to travel to the various displays, the Bureau would mail photograph exhibits to schools and organizations. Sets of photographs accompanied by a mimeographed lecture were loaned for two-week periods. For example, the Conquest of the Colorado set contained pictures of "Boulder, Parker, and Imperial Dams on the Colorado River, and All-American Canal."[57]

In summary, in addition to its own publications the Bureau of Reclamation endorsed and supported the positive use of its materials by independent authors and other parties. The policy resulted in a wide range of published materials from outside the agency that popularized the project's benefits and minimized the problems. The Bureau's staff also produced and distributed slides, prints, and transparencies, usually Glaha's, designed as propaganda and meant to convince the voting public of the advantages in keeping the agency well funded. The Bureau, always careful to place its efforts in the best possible light, regulated as best it could the use of its photographs, including creating and promoting new opportunities for Glaha's photographs to enhance the Boulder Canyon Project. In many instances, Glaha's photographs were fully exploited for their potential to augment government propaganda efforts. The same Glaha image could be used in varying contexts to evoke further responses. The aesthetic component of his images was integral to their value to the Bureau because of their persuasive power; photographs that were well crafted, visually dramatic, and aesthetically appealing were, as the Bureau propagandists were well aware, more likely to capture viewers' attention and, ultimately, affect their perceptions.

In addition to utilizing photographs to proactively advertise the project, the Bureau employed them to counteract negative publicity. For example, given the extreme temperature swings in the desert and the physical hazards at the dam site, there was justified public concern regarding the living and working conditions of the men. Six Companies, the employer of most of the men on the project and in the related service industries, was responsible for monitoring those conditions.[58] The men's needs, though, were not always met, as proved by an August 1931 mass strike of workers at the dam site. Some of the strikers' demands were an increased minimum daily wage, ice water provided on and off the job site until fountains with electric-coil coolers were installed, and a safety miner at each tunnel heading to provide first aid to injured workers.[59] Because Six Companies controlled the hiring and firing of employees on the project, it was the principal arbitrator. The Bureau monitored the strike to determine its effect on the smooth progress of the construction schedule. Two news items that appeared in the *Las Vegas Evening Review Journal* following the strike portrayed a highly positive situation in both Boulder City and at the dam site. The first, an article titled "Boulder City Is No Longer Man's Town: Family Life Comes to Stay at Government Community at Dam Site," stated: "Kiddies in rompers are playing with saws and hammers in sandy front yards, emulating the town-building example set by their elders. . . . Pajamaed lassies walk to the company commissary arm in arm to buy stationery and a 'coke.'"[60] The second item, a poem written by a worker on the dam, sang the praises of working and living on the project. His ode read in part:

> And the fallin' rocks can't scare us
> Nor the scorchin' rays of the sun
> We've rode the rods and brakebeams
> Ragged and on the bum
> And they gave us jobs and fed us
> When we needed it you bet
> And we all are truly thankful
> With no feelin' of regret.[61]

In the wake of the strike, both items were obviously meant to portray life in Boulder City and at the dam site as spiritually and economically ideal.

A less complimentary series of articles was published some five months after the strike. The series leveled criticisms against Six Companies' safety procedures—"Blasting has been carried out within 100 feet of where powder and fuses were stored together. On orders of my foreman, I've carried armloads of mixed powder and fuses into tunnels. If I had stumbled—goodby tunnel and about 80 men"—and wage levels—"Nowhere has the Six Companies been more criticized than for its wage scale."[62]

Surprisingly, there does not seem to have been any response by the Bureau to any of the criticisms leveled against the project. There are two plausible reasons for the lack of response. First, the Bureau may have decided to acknowledge that some aspects of the project, particularly employment and employee support issues, fell under the jurisdiction of Six Companies.[63] Therefore, the Bureau did not directly attempt to contradict any negative comments regarding those issues. Second, by quickly and efficiently completing the project despite any disruptions or negative press, the Bureau was using the rapidly completed structure as its best defense. The bottom line was the on-time and on-budget completion of a water management system. By sanctioning favorable publications and presentations, which relied heavily on photographs showing the swift and safe completion of the project, the Bureau was disseminating massive positive publicity regarding its role in the project while not giving credence to specific complaints made in public.[64]

The disastrous collapse of the St. Francis Dam undoubtedly further motivated the Bureau to proactively emphasize the safety of the project. William Mulholland built the dam in San Francisquito Canyon, forty miles northwest of Los Angeles, to provide water resources for the burgeoning city. When the dam crumbled at four minutes before midnight on March 12, 1928, the wall of water released from the dam killed in excess of 450 people, more than had lost their lives in the San Francisco earthquake. Margaret Leslie Davis investigated the catastrophe:

> The raging head of black water, moving at eighteen miles an hour, now swept through Castaic Junction and boiled into the dry Santa Clara River bed, heading west. The water whipped through the small towns of Piru, Fillmore, Bardsdale, and within three hours flooded Santa Paula, forty-two miles south and seventeen hundred feet lower than the dam. The murderous wall of water now dwindled to twenty-five feet but it still splintered three hundred homes in Santa Paula's southern section. The death and destruction continued, swirling through the hamlet of Saticoy, then across the Pacific Coast Highway into the Pacific Ocean between Oxnard and Ventura. . . . Steel bridges were smashed like tin cans, and acres of citrus and nut trees were uprooted. . . . When it was all over, parts of Ventura County lay under a seventy-foot thick blanket of slimy debris.[65]

The horrific event, which occurred just as construction of Hoover Dam was beginning, heightened public concern regarding the immediate and long-term stability of Hoover Dam. One of the best means the Bureau had of convincing the public that the dam would maintain its structural integrity was photographic images of the structure's careful and sound construction.

There is one other instance in which photographs by Glaha correspond to criticism leveled against the project: allegations that some of the project's hiring practices were racially discriminatory. While portions of the Bureau language that follows would today be considered racially derogatory, in the 1930s less consideration was paid to the terms in which race relations were discussed.

Early in the building program, Construction Engineer Young, in a confidential letter to Chief Engineer R. F. Walter, raised the issue of the hiring of Indians (Native Americans). He pointed out that preference for employment was given to citizens of the United States and to aliens who had "taken out their first papers of citizenship," and he therefore interpreted that "Indians are perhaps to be given first choice, since they are the original Americans."[66] He went on to state that "on account of climatic conditions, it is possible that Mexicans can be used to advantage during the warmer months."[67] Despite his racist comment, Young exhibited some empathy in regard to hiring Hispanic Americans when he wrote, "We must remember that it takes a Mexican and a white man about the same length of time to starve to death. The Mexican is here and he should be given some consideration."[68]

The hiring of persons of color, however, did not remain solely the subject of confidential correspondence. A letter from Joseph M. Dixon, the First Assistant Secretary in the Department of the Interior, to Fred Beckert, responded to Mr. Beckert's contention that "trustworthy citizens report having seen in the vicinity of the site of the Hoover dam a sign which reads: 'No White Men Need to Apply for Employment.'" Mr. Dixon stated that the matter was referred to Construction Engineer Young for investigation and report, and that no one in his office "can conceive of such an occurrence, except possibly some irresponsible outsider may have thought it a good joke to perpetrate on some moron who might take it seriously."[69]

Despite the First Secretary's flippant response, other individuals would soon express more substantiated complaints regarding minority employment practices. For example, three gentlemen writing on behalf of the "Colored working men of the U.S." stated to President Hoover that as of July 4, 1931, of the seven hundred to one thousand men at work on the dam, "there is not one colored man working in any capacity whatever."[70] The White House referred the letter to Acting Commissioner Dent, who responded that Six Companies had jurisdiction with respect to the employment situation and that the terms of its contract required it to give priority to ex-servicemen first and American citizens second. Beyond those two requirements, the employment practices were determined entirely by Six Companies.[71] A memo from Acting Construction Engineer John Page to the commissioner confirmed that as of July 27, 1931, there were no "negroes" employed on the project. Page went on to state, "The representatives of the Six Companies, Inc., have stated that while negroes would probably be desirable on account of the extreme heat, . . . the matter of housing and segregation has so far rendered it impractical to plan on their employment."[72]

By 1933, there were persons of color working on the dam. The call for hiring a greater percentage of minority individuals had not ceased, however. The National Association for the Advancement of Colored People (NAACP), in cooperation with the National Bar Association, wrote to Secretary of the Interior Ickes, requesting that he take action to see that "colored American citizens" were employed, that some of those hired be in positions other than laborers at the minimum wage, and that "colored people" be permitted to reside in Boulder City.[73] In his response to the NAACP, Commissioner Mead reiterated the position that hiring policies were determined by the contractor, Six Companies, and that the construction of separate housing and mess facilities for what would be a small number of employees was "hardly feasible."[74]

Indians Employed on the Construction of Hoover Dam as High Scalers. This group includes one Yaqui, one Crow, one Navajo, and six Apaches. October 5, 1932.

Negroes Employed as Drillers on the Construction of Hoover Dam. October 3, 1932.

The concerns regarding the hiring of persons of color directly relate to photographic images produced by the Bureau. There are two Glaha photographs, both taken in October 1932, that address the issue of minority employment. The first picture shows a group of nine Native Americans employed on the construction of Hoover Dam as high scalers, *Indians Employed on the Construction of Hoover Dam as High Scalers.* The second is of a group of six African Americans employed as drillers, *Negroes Employed as Drillers on the Construction of Hoover Dam.* Both images present their subjects as individuals with dignity. The tasks each group performed are alluded to: the Native Americans are posed on the canyon rim, and four of the men have ropes tied around their waists; the African Americans are grouped with three drills.

There are two curious elements to these images. The first is that the posing of groups of workmen was atypical for Glaha. While he did take other images of workmen, the proportion of those images was quite small in comparison to the entire body of his work. Further, no other photograph has been found in which he posed groups of workers in a similar fashion. Other Glaha photographs show men *in situ*, performing their assigned tasks. One practical reason for posing the two groups was that by having the individuals stop working and face the camera, he could better document their ethnicity.[75]

The second curious element is that no instance has been found of these two images being published. Why were the images made and not reproduced? The answer to that question may be similar to the stance taken by the Bureau in regard to other criticisms leveled against it: the Bureau deferred to Six Companies' jurisdiction, in this case regarding the hiring of employees, and chose to emphasize the work completed on the dam regardless of the ethnicity of the workers responsible for the dam's erection.

In conclusion, the Bureau of Reclamation sought to advertise Hoover Dam as a structurally and economically sound venture. Photographs, alone and with text, conveyed the dam's structural, fiscal, and commercial potential. Although the Bureau generally avoided or ignored criticisms of its methods and policies, it proactively circulated visual and written propaganda that represented the project and, ultimately, its mission in the most positive manner possible.

6 GLAHA'S CONTRIBUTION SPREADS BEYOND THE DAM

In the fall of 1936, Glaha, then a recognized authority in the field of photography, was invited by the Artists' Cooperative Gallery in San Francisco to deliver three lectures on photography and to mount an exhibit of some of his industrial images. In a letter to Acting Commissioner John Page, Glaha expressed his desire to fulfill the Gallery's requests. In describing the Gallery, he stated that it "corresponds to the Art Students' League of New York."[1] Glaha further bolstered his argument in favor of his participation by adding, "The other lecturers before the photographic forum are men of reputation and the entire cooperative plan has had the support of civic leaders from the first so there is no question of the value or dignity of the endeavor."[2] Glaha doubtless knew that the exposure he would receive at the exhibition would enhance his reputation in the field as well as providing him introductions to other photographic professionals and laypersons supportive of his craft. The Bureau readily recognized the dual exposure for itself and for Glaha. As Acting Commissioner Page stated in his letter of approval of Glaha's lectures and exhibition, "To have him fulfill this engagement will reflect credit to the Department and the Bureau, since the exhibit will, of course, carry placards bearing the names of the Department of the Interior and the Bureau of Reclamation."[3]

Glaha's lectures at the Artists' Cooperative Gallery must have been a personal and professional success; he was asked to instruct, from January 4 to June 7, 1937, at the Art Students' League of San Francisco. Glaha was listed in the school's catalog (along with fellow instructors Ansel Adams, Horace Bristol, Imogen Cunningham, Dorothea Lange, and Roger Sturtevant) as offering a photographic forum comprised of a "lecture course with individual criticism."[4]

In addition to his lectures and teaching, Glaha's Hoover Dam photographs served in several other ways as examples for other artists: as an introduction to a new stylistic approach, as studies for their artworks, and as the impetus to examine topics they might not ordinarily attempt.

For example, Glaha guided the photographer Margaret Bourke-White through Boulder Dam, for which she thanked him by autographing a copy of her *Eyes on Russia*, "So delighted to have a chance to autograph this after a magnificent day at Boulder Dam for which I have largely to thank Ben Glaha, Very Gratefully, Margaret Bourke-White, Nov. 21 '35."[5]

Bourke-White's *Eyes on Russia* photographs were among her earliest and most seminal work. In them, the discrepancy between her and Glaha's stylistic approaches is evident in that she carefully arranged figures in some of the photographs. Regarding Bourke-White's use of people in her Russian photographs, Vicki Goldberg claims: "Margaret did not merely report what she saw but arranged it to the best possible advantage. If she wanted two workers in a scene where only one existed, she would scour the factory for someone who would look right in the picture. People were still 'types' for her, or accessories, but she thought that Russians at least fell easily into dramatic poses; she worked on their portrayals with them or composed them to look better."[6] Particularly in his art exhibition prints, Glaha rarely included people, except perhaps for scale, did not stage images, and concentrated on distilling the pure architectonic elements of the dam. As a result, he may have offered Bourke-White some unique insights into photographing such a structure. In fact, her subsequent image *Fort Peck Dam, Montana* (1936), the first cover of *Life* magazine (November 23, 1936), shares with Glaha's work an attempt to reduce the structure to pure, almost abstract, forms. Additionally, the people in Bourke-White's cover are included for scale, not for any statement of worker typology.

Even more direct evidence of Glaha's influence can be found in those instances where his photographs served as studies for the works of other artists. Bureau correspondence exists in which the use of his work as artists' studies is readily acknowledged. For example, in a letter from Walker Young to Commissioner Mead, Young stated, regarding a body of sixty prints Glaha had compiled while covering the construction process, "A number of these prints have been used as a basis for drawings and paintings by artists who have visited the project."[7] One such artist was the architect William Woollett, who produced a series of sketches and lithographs of the dam's construction. Woollett attended the University of Minnesota, was a draftsman in the New York offices of James Gamble Rogers and Alexander B. Throwbridge, and worked with his father, William Lee Woollett, a Los Angeles architect, until 1930.[8] After assisting his father, he began a series of works in which he recorded the progress of large construction projects in the southwestern United States, including Boulder Dam.[9] Woollett exhibited and published the resulting construction project sketches and lithographs.

Some of Woollett's sketches and lithographs of the Boulder Dam construction process were, in this author's opinion, based on Glaha photographs.[10] A memorandum from Construction Engineer Walker Young to the Commissioner requests that a specific selection of photographs be sent to Woollett: "These are to be used by Mr. Woollett in preparation for a group of etchings."[11] The Bureau was willing to comply with Woollett's request for photographs on which to base his works because, as Walker Young stated, "The work he is doing tends to reflect credit on the activities of the Bureau of Reclamation in

Fort Peck Dam, Montana. Margaret Bourke-White. 1936. This was the first cover of *Life* magazine, November 23, 1936.

construction of the dam."[12] The Bureau, which was quite selective about the manner in which its project was portrayed, respected Woollett's work and believed that his art promoted the project in a positive manner. Woollett sought financial support from the government for his efforts.[13]

An example of a Woollett lithograph bearing a close resemblance to a Glaha photograph is his *Penstock Towers* (before 1935). It is strikingly similar to Glaha's *The Nevada Intake Towers at Boulder Dam* (before 1935). The point of view, framing, and details, such as catwalks and gantryways, are nearly identical. The only differences are that Woollett has cropped his image slightly on the right-hand edge, and he has placed one of the eight-cubic-yard concrete buckets being lowered into the canyon in a slightly different position than in the photograph.[14]

As another example, Woollett's *Diversion Tunnel Interior at Junction with Spillway Shaft* (before 1935) is essentially identical to Glaha's *Looking Upstream through the Upstream Tunnel Plug Construction in Diversion Tunnel No. 3* (1934).[15] The only real difference in the two works is that while the people in the photograph appear to have lined up adjacent to the left rear of the truck, Woollett has depicted the figures actively employed throughout the scene. Other details—such as the wood strewn in the lower right-hand corner, the pipes lying alongside the truck, and the hook descending from the overhead track—are arranged similarly.

A final example of the correlation between Glaha's photographs and Woollett's works of art is Woollett's *General View Looking Upriver* (before 1935), which shows a huge section of a penstock tunnel lining being swung over the canyon rim, where it will be lowered and taken to its position inside the walls far below.[16] The lithograph strongly corresponds to Glaha's *Lowering a 140-Ton Penstock Section into the Canyon over the 150-Ton-Capacity Cableway* (before 1935) in its point of view and framing.[17]

A final example of the influence of Glaha's photographs is an instance in which his pictures served as the impetus for an artist to examine a topic for which he was not generally known. Glaha's photographs of Boulder Dam were most likely the model on which the photographer Ansel Adams based his own studies of the dam. While Adams had certainly photographed architectural structures before, he was primarily known for his landscape studies. A strong correlation between the two photographers' images of the dam points to an attempt by Adams to emulate Glaha's approach.

Adams was familiar enough with Glaha's photographs to present a lecture on Glaha's work in conjunction with the 1935 DeYoung Museum exhibition of his Hoover Dam photographs. In 1941 and 1942, Adams produced a series of images of Boulder Dam. The Adams photographs are compiled in a folio titled "Photographs of National Parks by Ansel Adams, 1933–42."[18] Adams's images bear a striking resemblance to photographs taken by Glaha between 1934 and 1938. For example, his *Boulder Dam* (1941), showing the top of the dam with transmission lines on the left and mountains in the background, bears a resemblance to Glaha's *Boulder Dam, a Portion of Intake Towers* (1938). Glaha's view is quite similar to Adams's except that it is taken from a higher vantage point. Even more strikingly similar are Adams's *Boulder Dam* (1942), a vertical close-up of the dam face, and Glaha's *The Crest of the Dam as Seen from the Arizona Abutment* (1936). Finally, a strong correlation can be seen between Adams's *Boulder Dam Power Units* (1941) and Glaha's *Bureau of Power and Light of Los Angeles Switchyard* (1938).

In each instance, Glaha and Adams show similarities in their point of view, camera angle, and framing of a portion of the dam and its appurtenant works. Their images, though, are more than photographs of some element of the dam; they celebrate the dam's geometry and its placement within an organic setting. Because the similarities between the two photographers' works are so striking, and owing to the fact that Glaha produced his images prior to Adams's, it is arguable that Glaha's images served as an impetus for Adams's and, further, that Adams was stylistically influenced by Glaha.

When Adams's studies are examined more closely, it can be further argued that although, like Glaha, Adams produced some notable images of the dam, unlike Glaha he was not able to capture the power and grace of the dam's geometry within the desert setting. For example, Adams's version of the power unit is an oblique view of the components with a fairly undramatic sky in the background. Glaha also photographs the components from an oblique angle, but he places the left-hand part of the structure in the immediate foreground. The proximity of the left-hand part of the structure engages the viewer more directly with the image. Further, in his photographs Glaha gives a more informative glimpse of the surrounding terrain and combines it with a more dramatic sky, which together create a balanced juxtaposition against the foreground geometry.

Likewise, Adams's photograph of the dam face is an attempt to balance the smoother contours of the dam structure with the textural irregularities of the natural setting. Adams has contrived to underscore the juxtaposition by contrasting the concrete surface of the utility tower on the left with the segment of canyon wall on the right; however, the comparison is diluted by the repeating curvilinear horizontal lines on the large expanse of the dam's face. In short, Adams has attempted to incorporate several visually interesting aspects of the dam into his image, and in so doing he has created a photograph in which there is a confusion instead of an extraction of contrasting elements. Glaha created an image that incorporates fewer elements and thereby makes a stronger statement. Whereas Adams contrasted the dam's concrete with the surrounding natural terrain in the upper left, center, and lower right portions of his picture, Glaha makes the same comparison only in the upper third of his print. In so doing, Glaha conveys the power of the structure, which in this case is enhanced by the repeating horizontal lines of the concrete pourings and by the spare yet forceful mountains in the background. Despite the fact that Glaha has incorporated less of the dam face than Adams, by framing the utility

Penstock Towers. William Woollett. Before 1935. Lithograph.

The Nevada Intake Towers at Boulder Dam. Before 1935.

Diversion Tunnel Interior at Junction with Spillway Shaft. William Woollett. Before 1935. Lithograph.

Looking Upstream through the Upstream Tunnel Plug Construction in Diversion Tunnel No. 3. This view shows the intersection of the inclined tunnel from the intake tower with the present diversion tunnel and the downstream face of the upstream section of the tunnel plug. June 27, 1934.

General View Looking Upriver. William Woollett. Before 1935. Lithograph.

Lowering a 140-Ton Penstock Section into the Canyon over the 150-Ton-Capacity Cableway. Before 1935.

Boulder Dam. Ansel Adams. 1941.

Boulder Dam, a Portion of Intake Towers, the Rim Tower for Units N-1 to N-4, from the Elk's Flagpole Point.
April 15, 1938.

Boulder Dam. Ansel Adams. 1942.

The Crest of the Dam as Seen from the Arizona Abutment, Showing the Arizona Elevator and Utility Towers.
September 17, 1936.

Boulder Dam Power Units. Ansel Adams. 1941.

Bureau of Power and Light of Los Angeles Switchyard. April 15, 1938.

View Looking Upstream through the Nevada Spillway Channel from the Portal of the Inclined Tunnel.
April 13, 1938.

tower in the right foreground, Glaha anchors the structure within the image, thereby giving his dam face a strength and presence not found in Adams's photograph. Finally, because he imbues his background mountains with a greater verticality than Adams does, Glaha's surrounding terrain is more proportionately balanced with the dam's architectonic mass.

Yet while Ansel Adams has long been recognized as a key figure in photography, Ben Glaha has yet to receive accolades equivalent to Adams's. Nevertheless, as the above comparisons reveal, Glaha was a significant contributor and influence in terms of architectural photography.[19]

In conclusion, what Glaha does in his aestheticizing images of the dam is make a powerful statement celebrating and glorifying the formal beauty of the dam's construction. Once the tools, trucks, and scaffolds are gone, photographs of the completed dam convey power in the structure's soaring lines and beauty in its geometric forms. Glaha's clear statement with his images is that man has triumphed over extreme climatic conditions, the vagaries of the river, and the geology of the land. It is significant that in these images the smooth, flowing lines and volumes of concrete dominate the picture plane. In *View Looking Upstream through the Nevada Spillway Channel*, for example, flowing undulations of poured concrete command the image. The rough canyon walls in the background function in textural juxtaposition to the concrete, but it is the smooth surfaces and repeating lines of the man-made elements that are given precedence. It is as if the chasm of the spillway functions as a new river replacing the old; whereas the old Colorado ran wild and irregular, this new waterway is controlled and symmetrical. The human figure leaning against the railing in the upper right-hand corner serves to remind us of the fact that this is a man-made "river," yet it is almost inconceivable that so tiny a figure could have commanded such an achievement. The allusion, therefore, is not only to man's physical efforts in creating the structure but also to the technological prowess he commanded to complete the task.

Like other artists celebrating the Machine Aesthetic, Glaha is in no way critical of the dam either in its design or in its function. His images do not question the right of such a monolithic structure to exist in the midst of nature's domain. Rather, the manner in which his images give supremacy to the steel and concrete speaks to his absolute belief in the rightness of their purpose.

7

CONTEMPORARY PHOTOGRAPHY
Water in the West Today

In the second half of the nineteenth century, photographers from the East ventured west to photograph the vast, untamed lands. A hundred years later, photographers continue to explore the western landscape, although undeveloped lands are the exception instead of the norm. In response to the pervasive development, the current aim of photographers and other artists is to convey the impact of mankind's hand upon the landscape. In particular, artists have called into question the ecological impact of water management systems, particularly dams. At the time that Glaha was photographing the rise of Hoover Dam, dams were seen as natural—indeed, aesthetic—additions to the landscape. Today, however, the pictures photographers are producing reflect a more critical stance regarding alterations to the natural environment.

Art historian Richard Guy Wilson perceived in one image the coalescence of a man-made construct with the environment; he wrote regarding Margaret Bourke-White's photograph *Fort Peck Dam, Montana*, on the inaugural cover of *Life*: "Projected is a gigantic machine, a sublime construction of man that transcends topography to become a geological feature."[1] To allow that an unabashedly inorganic, monolithic creation of concrete and steel could be presented as a rightfully and naturally occurring part of the landscape is an extreme embrace of the machine in the garden. Moreover, the image speaks to a time when dams were hailed as a natural and rightful means by which mankind could conform nature to its own ends.

More recently, however, the placement of dams, canals, and waterways in the natural terrain has been reconsidered. Such structures, which were formerly perceived as integrated into the landscape, are beginning to be viewed as intrusions. For example, Secretary of the Interior Bruce Babbitt, "wants to restore, if in small measure, the ecological balance that existed before Interior's Bureau of Reclamation began its nearly 100 years of dam-building."[2] Babbitt has proposed dismantling the Glines Canyon and Elwha dams in Washington state's Olympic National Park. (Glines Canyon and Elwha are not Bureau of Reclamation dams, although the Bureau is involved with studies concerning their removal.) Removal of the dams would, in the Interior Department's opinion, restore some of the nation's most significant and currently endangered fisheries. Dismantling the dams would directly oppose previous Bureau activity, which, "While slaking the West's nearly unquenchable thirst for water and electricity . . . has also helped wipe out 90% of the West's salmon and altered the habitats of countless other species that hover close to extinction."[3]

The Bureau of Reclamation has attempted to redress one dam's ecological consequences with the installation of the $80 million Shasta temperature control device on the upstream face of Shasta Dam in California. The mechanism will provide a constant flow of cold water in the Sacramento River below the dam. In 1976–1977, thousands of winter-run Chinook salmon were killed when water discharged from Shasta exceeded the maximum temperature that can be tolerated by the fish and their eggs. Reporting for the *San Francisco Examiner*, Eric Brazil stated, "For Reclamation, which until recently regarded dam building as its primary mission, the cooling device is a big switch—a high-profile project driven by environmental considerations."[4]

Glaha could never have predicted such a complete reversal of attitude toward water resource management. His images typify an era when landscape photography was usually less about the landscape and more about the multitude of ways mankind had exerted its domination over the natural terrain. Today, however, just as government policy regarding the land is changing, so is the emphasis that landscape photographers are placing on man's relation to the land. Whereas Glaha sought to publicize the benefits of man's orchestration of natural resources, today photographers are taking a critical stance against such intervention. Robert Webb, who compared photographs of the Grand Canyon taken in 1889 and 1890 with his rephotography of the same places nearly a hundred years later, wrote:

> The most crucial change in the geomorphology and ecology of Grand Canyon during the past century occurred in 1963. The closure of Glen Canyon Dam ended any pretense of a natural riverine environment in Grand Canyon. The second most important change was the closure of Hoover Dam below the canyon in 1935, which caused the last 40 miles of free-flowing river in Grand Canyon to become the delta of what was at that time the largest reservoir in the world, Lake Mead. Now, with the turn of some valves, humans can manipulate, among other things, sandbars, rapids, riparian vegetation, and wildlife habitat.[5]

The change in the focus of attention for landscape photographers can be traced to the marked escalation in the development of the West in the latter half of the twentieth century and the burgeoning ecology movement of the 1970s. John Szarkowski elegantly paraphrased the situation in his 1974 introduction to photographer Robert Adams's book *The New West*: "As Americans we are scarred by the dream of innocence. In our hearts we still believe that the only truly beautiful landscape is an unopposed one. So to wash our eyes of the depressing evidence we have raced deeper and deeper into the wilderness . . . to see and claim a section of God's own garden before our fellows arrive to spoil it. Now we are beginning to realize that there is no wilderness left."[6]

Adams's words are visually illustrated by the juxtaposition of an unattributed nineteenth-century image of the Grand Canyon and Lewis Baltz's *Foundation Construction, Many Warehouses* (1973–1974). In the nineteenth-century image, the blue sensitivity of the wet-plate process leaves the horizon and the lands beyond it only barely perceptible. The fading topography in the photograph's background is a metaphor for the seemingly endless acres of undeveloped land stretching into the distance. The figure in the right middle ground, by pointing into the distance, invites the viewer to proceed with him into the virgin lands ahead.

In Baltz's photograph, however, mankind's domination over the land is virtually absolute. Man-made materials replace the ground; there is only a nominal association with an open landscape. The soil, unscathed in the older photograph, now bears the marks of tractor tires. In summary, on the one hand, man stands facing westward into virtually endless miles of undeveloped terrain; on the other, he is both at the literal limit—for we are at the far western edge of California—and the metaphorical limit of Manifest Destiny. Lest we think, however, that Baltz's photograph, with its carefully created and controlled space, is a fluke, we only have to remember Bourke-White's *Fort Peck Dam, Montana*, where the substitution of monolithic concrete for monolithic rock is complete.

With human habitation comes industrial and suburban development, in turn begetting waste and detritus that appear at the site of, and sometimes miles from, their sources. Lewis Baltz poignantly illustrated this fact in his 1981–1983 series "San Quentin Point." The series depict how one of the then undeveloped plots of land in the San Francisco Bay area bore the marks and debris of the development and consumerism surrounding it.

In another study, a group of photographers joined to produce "Second View: The Rephotographic Survey Project," which sought to scientifically determine just how much change had taken place in the West since it was first photographically documented by the western territories survey parties of the late 1800s. By returning to the sites and approximating the vantage points of their predecessors, Mark Klett, Ellen Manchester, JoAnn Verburg, Gordon Bushaw, and Rick Dingus attempted to rephotograph the monuments and views taken by photographers such as William Henry Jackson and Timothy O'Sullivan. In those instances where roads, power lines, and TV antennas had not arrived, the contemporary images appeared remarkably similar to their predecessors. However, views seemingly unsullied by modern contrivances are often deceiving. Although not visible in the photographs, often campgrounds and rock music were firmly established just out of sight. Further, Robert Adams's book

Grand Canyon, Arizona (?). Unattributed stereograph.

Foundation Construction, Many Warehouses, 2892 Kelvin, Irvine. Lewis Baltz. 1973–1974.

The New West: Landscapes along the Colorado Front Range provided glimpses of a state where formerly virgin terrain had been abraded for the placement of house frames, mobile homes, and gas stations.[7]

The new western suburban settlements required that their inhabitants be fed, and agriculture, particularly in California's Central Valley, took on the challenge. Farming became "agribusiness," and the demand for water increased exponentially. The Bureau of Reclamation was ready for the challenge, and its system of dams, canals, and waterways helped make areas such as the Central Valley a "fruit and vegetable basket" for the entire nation. In fact, up to 80 percent of California's water use is for agricultural irrigation. Water allocation in California is such a volatile issue that former U.S. senator Bill Bradley (D-N.J.) laid the foundation for a bill intended to balance the controversial division of water between urban and agricultural users. Why would a New Jersey Democrat take such an interest in California water resources? Perhaps Bradley thought to campaign one day for the United States presidency and was well aware of the financial and political clout of potential California agribusiness constituents.[8]

The politicization of western water issues continues to filter into historical writing and landscape photography. A consortium composed of historians, writers, and landscape photographers, the Water in the West Project, has focused its attention on the sociopolitical ramifications of western water management. In their first publication, *A River Too Far: The Past and Future of the Arid West*, Joseph Finkhouse summarizes the consortium's goal in relation to what the members perceive as the current state of the arid West: "Our intention is to question, to challenge, to learn, for in the desert the issues of water and irrigation must influence the entire fabric of a society. From the wagon trains to the modern subdivisions, Westerners have tried to control rather than adapt to their environment. It is now mandatory that we learn from our history in the desert and wisely manage the West's most valuable resource."[9]

The writings in the book seek to reevaluate the nature of our perceptions and actions in regard to the desert. Patricia Limerick, for example, examines what we perceive as myth versus reality regarding our arid lands. She finds that our initial attempts to dominate the desert have given us what amounts to a false sense of mastery over that terrain. She states, "The existence of a final, resolved state of mastery and appreciation is simply illusory."[10] What she refers to as the "alchemy of irrigation" has been, as the term implies, a fruitless attempt to make something precious, verdure, out of a base element, the desert.[11] Such a stance is, of course, antipodal to that of the Bureau of Reclamation. The Bureau historically stood for the mastery of water resources by regulating, storing, and diverting them, and thereby enabling cultivation of the arid landscape.

In another chapter, John McPhee juxtaposes the Bureau of Reclamation's stance against that of conservationists. Specifically, he contrasts the position of former United States commissioner of reclamation Floyd E. Dominy with that of conservationist David Brower. Dominy's position was that the environment should be altered in the service of man: "Let's use our environment. Nature changes the environment every day of our lives—why shouldn't we change it? We're part of nature." Brower has united "sportsmen, ecologists, wilderness preservers, park advocates, and so forth" against Bureau projects such as the one that would have inundated portions of Dinosaur National Monument. Brower has stated, perhaps only quasi-facetiously, "The Bureau of Reclamation engineers are like beavers. They can't stand the sight of running water."[12] Secretary Babbitt's proposal to dismantle the two Washington state dams rings as a victory for conservationists and supports the position that man's mastery of arid lands is merely illusory.

The photographs in *A River Too Far*, produced by Water in the West photographers, eloquently illustrate how our relationship with water resources, and landscape photography, have changed in recent years. For example, Robert Dawson's *Cracked Mud and Vineyard, near Arvin, California* (1985), from the Great Central Valley Project photographs, speaks to decisions made as to which lands will receive water and which will not. In this instance, nonnative plants are irrigated at the expense of the surrounding terrain. Dawson has carefully framed his photograph so that the parched land in the foreground looms large in relation to the lush vineyards beyond. The implied result is that the widening fissures in the mud threaten to devour the delicate vines. The allusion in Dawson's image is to the precarious line between irrigation and aridity: How long can we infuse water into areas that are normally parched? The implication inherent in many of these photographs is that our perception of our ability to regulate and allocate water resources wisely is tenuous at best.

Finally, in one of the most telling images in terms of juxtaposing Glaha's work with contemporary landscape images, Martin Stupich photographed Hoover Dam. Stupich's photograph, *Hoover Dam from Roadway, South into Boulder Canyon* (1989), does not, as Glaha's photographs did, celebrate the sculptural beauty and physical strength of a dam nestled in its environment. Instead, Stupich focuses on the top of the powerhouse so that the concrete and electrical transformers are set in sharp opposition to the river and the canyon walls. Whereas Glaha's photographs portray the dam as rightfully situated within the canyon, here the dam resembles a concrete plug wedged into the natural terrain. Least emphasized in Stupich's image is the Colorado River, the impetus for the dam. Stupich's photograph reiterates an important aspect of the dam's existence: it is a large, man-made construct placed within nature for the purpose of generating electrical power.

In summary, the manner in which the landscape is portrayed photographically has changed since Glaha created his images of Hoover Dam. While his more aesthetic photographs, with their emphasis on formalism, are not dissimilar to images produced today, the sociopolitical context within which his images were conceived has altered dramatically. Glaha's clout as a historical figure lies not in his foreshadowing the change that was to take place in landscape photography but in his encapsula-

Cracked Mud and Vineyard, near Arvin, California. Robert Dawson. From the Great Central Valley Project.
Copyright 1985.

Hoover Dam from Roadway, South into Boulder Canyon. Martin Stupich. 1989.

tion, within his Hoover Dam images, of the social climate in which they were created. Better than any others of his time, his photographs conveyed, and in so doing spread, the belief that the land required mankind's intervention before its natural resources could be utilized. In Glaha's images, arid lands could, and therefore must, be made green. It was not acceptable, given the availability of modern technology, to coexist with arid terrain. Instead, the land found its fulfillment only when subjugated to mankind's will. In Depression-era America, the country was trying to pull itself to its feet, and Hoover Dam was a firm handhold. Given the potential of providing water and thereby irrigating crops, which in turn fed people, who in turn supported commerce and industry, concerns about how the land was altered by man's manipulations were not considered.

Today, however, development in the western United States has grown to such proportions that there is fear that there will not be enough water to meet future private and commercial needs. More important, the manner in which existing resources are being utilized has been called into question. For example, years of crop irrigation have had the unexpected side effect of transporting pesticides in run-off water, and the dams responsible for that irrigation have altered the temperature, flow, and aquatic life in the rivers they were built to control.

Contemporary landscape photographers, unlike Glaha, have elected to examine the dichotomy between past and future utilization of water resources. Whereas Glaha stood close to the theme of man's determined alteration of the natural terrain, the Water in the West photographers have taken a step backward in order to examine the entire context in which the naturally arid West has been altered to suit not its natural purposes but those of mankind. The result of their and others' findings may be a radical rethinking of the extent to which the arid West is managed. As a result, Hoover Dam may not be permitted to stand for its projected life of one hundred years.

Glaha's photographs, however, will outlast the dam. And like the images of his nineteenth-century predecessors, his photographs will remain as interpretations not only of the land but also of mankind's intentions toward it.

NOTES

Abbreviations: NARA-RMR: National Archives and Records Administration, Rocky Mountain Region; NARA-W: National Archives, Washington, D.C.; RG: Record Group.

Chapter 1. The Shovel and the Camera

1. Robert D. McCraken, *Las Vegas: The Great American Playground* (Fort Collins, Colo.: Marion Street, 1996), 35.

2. For further reading regarding the geologist, see Peter Wild, *Clarence King* (Boise, Idaho: Boise State University, 1981) or Thurman Wilkins, *Clarence King: A Biography* (New York: Macmillan, 1958). King's memoirs are *The Helmet of Mambrino* (New York: G. P. Putnam's Sons, 1904).

3. David O. Woodbury, *The Colorado Conquest* (New York: Dodd, Mead, 1941), 28.

4. Regarding Powell's explorations, see *The Professor Goes West: Illinois Wesleyan University Reports of Major John Wesley Powell's Explorations, 1867–1874* (Bloomington: Illinois Wesleyan University Press, 1954).

5. Ibid, 22.

6. *Water: Changing Values and Needs for People and Nature* (Arlington, Va., and Washington, D.C.: National Water Resources Association and Bureau of Reclamation, n.d.), 6 (pamphlet).

7. Ibid, 8.

8. Cited in Joseph E. Stevens, *Hoover Dam: An American Adventure* (Norman: University of Oklahoma Press, 1988), 17–18. Stevens provides a thorough account of the irrigation and settlement of the Imperial Valley and of the legislation leading up to and resulting in the construction of Hoover Dam, pp. 10–19.

9. Even though the dam was built in Black Canyon, the name Boulder, from the Boulder Canyon Project Act, had become so closely associated with the dam that the name Boulder stuck. In September 1930 the name was changed to Hoover Dam in honor of President Herbert Hoover. However, on May 18, 1933, under the subsequent presidential administration, Secretary of the Interior Harold L. Ickes made the political decision to change the name back to Boulder Dam. Finally, on April 30, 1947, the name Hoover Dam was reinstated by a joint resolution of Congress. Ibid., 173–175, 290.

10. For a thorough discussion of the Bureau contract, Six Companies, and the bids submitted, see ibid., 34–46.

11. Ibid., 260.

12. Bureau of Reclamation. For further reading regarding the Bureau of Reclamation, see Brookings Institution, Institute for Government Research, *The U.S. Reclamation Service: Its History, Activities and Organization* (New York: D. Appleton, 1919); Doris Ostrander Dawdy, *Congress in Its Wisdom: The Bureau of Reclamation and the Public Interest* (Boul-

der, Colo.: Westview Press, 1989); and U.S. Department of the Interior, Bureau of Reclamation, *Historical Information on Bureau of Reclamation Hydroelectric Facilities, 1902–1962* (Denver: The Bureau, 1990).

13. L. M. Holt, "How the Reclamation Service Is Robbing the Settler," *Overland Monthly and Out West Magazine* 50 (November 1907): 510–512.

14. Dawdy, *Congress in Its Wisdom*, 9, 11.

15. Ibid, 11.

16. Ibid, 25. In her text, Dawdy also examines Davis's personal and professional ambitions and concludes that, his belief in the Reclamation Act aside, Davis was perhaps more concerned about his alliances with William Mulholland and other influential Californians. Additionally, she states, "he initiated more projects than could be completed within a reasonable period of time, succumbed to political pressure in site selection, failed to provide drainage facilities where they were needed, and made expensive engineering errors which the beneficiaries of the projects were expected to pay in addition to what they had contracted to pay" (ibid., 24). Such poor site and drainage decisions were later to have grave ecological effects, such as the mobilization of selenium into irrigation drainwater in California's Kesterson National Wildlife Refuge. For a discussion of the problem, see ibid., 4, 72–75. Since the advent of the ecology movement in the 1970s, much closer attention has been paid to all manner of ecological impacts from water diversion and storage facilities.

17. Richard L. Berkman and W. Kip Viscusi, *Ralph Nader's Study Group Report on the Bureau of Reclamation: Damming the West* (New York: Grossman, 1973), 5.

18. Ibid, 7.

19. Dawdy, *Congress in Its Wisdom*, 3, 31.

20. Pete Daniel et al., *Official Images: New Deal Photography* (Washington, D.C.: Smithsonian Institution Press, 1987), ix.

21. Betty Houchin Winfield, *FDR and the News Media* (Urbana: University of Illinois Press, 1990), 87. Thomas P. Hughes, in his book *American Genesis: A Century of Invention and Technological Enthusiasm, 1870–1970* (New York: Viking, 1989), and Jordan A. Schwarz, in his book *The New Dealers: Power Politics in the Age of Roosevelt* (New York: Alfred A. Knopf, 1993), both delve into what, specifically, the New Dealers hoped to achieve from balanced regional economic development to an American middle class hungry for electrical appliances. See Hughes, 356–357, and Schwarz, xii, 345.

22. Daniel et al., *Official Images*, 36.

23. Ibid., 37.

24. For a thorough discussion of the images, see Ulrich Keller, *The Building of the Panama Canal in Historic Photographs* (New York: Dover, 1983).

Chapter 2. The Unique Talents of Ben Glaha Suit the Task

1. Wesley Nell, Glaha's nephew, stated in an April 28, 1990 interview with the author that he believed Glaha may have been married at one time. There is no information that this was the case, and Glaha's death certificate specifies that he was "never married."

2. Letter dated 2/5/17 from Glaha to his mother, postmarked New Orleans, from the collection of George Rinhart, who kindly made available to me his collection of Glaha's letters and personal artifacts.

3. Letter dated 12/2/17 from Glaha to his mother, postmarked Camp Pike, Little Rock, Arkansas, from the collection of George Rinhart.

4. Letters dated 8/27/17 and 9/4/18, from Glaha to his mother, postmarked Fort Logan, Houston, Texas, from the collection of George Rinhart.

5. Typewritten copy of "1916 Senior Farewell" text, courtesy of Wesley Nell; letter dated 10/12/17, from Glaha to his mother, postmarked Fort Douglas, Salt Lake City, from the collection of George Rinhart.

6. Jean R. Page, a resident of Boulder City during the dam's construction, wrote this recollection of Glaha in a 5/28/92 letter to the author.

7. B. D. Glaha, "Boulder City Boasts a Band," *The Reclamation Era* 23 (September 1932): 155.

8. Ben Glaha, "Boulder Dam: The Photography of Engineering Works," *U.S. Camera* no. 2 (January–February 1939): 18.

9. Letter dated 8/13/17, from his mother to Glaha at Fort Douglas, Salt Lake City, postmarked Fort Madison, Iowa, from the collection of George Rinhart.

10. Letter dated 3/?/19, from Glaha to his mother, postmarked Fort Sheridan, Illinois, from the collection of George Rinhart. Regarding his background in photography, Glaha would later write, "I had been a lifelong amateur." See Glaha, "Photography of Engineering Works," 18.

11. Letter dated 4/5/19, from Glaha to his mother, postmarked Camp Nicholls, Louisiana, from the collection of George Rinhart.

12. Newsletter, *The Muster Plaster*, Camp Hospital, Camp Meade, Maryland, dated 2/13/20, from the collection of George Rinhart

13. The letter, dated 8/9/24, is from Gocko [Jack?] in Pueblo, Colorado, and is addressed to BB ("Big Brother"), in care of the *Evening Democrat*, Fort Madison, Iowa. The letter is from the collection of George Rinhart. The clipping states in part, "L. T. McNerney, who has held the position of editor of the Evening Democrat . . . has resigned. . . . McNerney's position as editor of the Evening Democrat will be taken by Bernard Glaha, who has been connected with the paper as city editor for the past nine months." Clipping courtesy of Wesley Nell.

14. It is possible that between 1926 and 1930 Glaha attended college. In 1919 he had written home that he did not plan to continue his formal education: "A college education is, of course, out of the question. . . . Too much time has passed from the time I last saw the inside of a school for a college education to be practicable to me. . . . [W]hat I do and what I make of myself I am going to do entirely by my own efforts." The fact, however, that upon his return to the Bureau he was employed as a senior engineering draftsman suggests some sort of formal training. Letter dated 1/19/19, from Glaha to his mother, postmarked Camp Logan, from the collection of George Rinhart.

15. Letter dated 2/26/32, from Chief Engineer R. F. Walter to Construction Engineer Walker R. Young; National Archives and Records Administration, Rocky Mountain Region, Record Group 115. Also letter dated 5/12/32, from Richard B. Lyman to Young; NARA-RMR, RG 115.

16. University of Nevada, Las Vegas, Manis Collection, MC-6-13.

17. Letter dated 11/23/31, from Young to Elwood Mead, Commissioner of the Bureau of Reclamation; National Archives, Washington, D.C. (NARA-W), RG 115. I am not certain what, specifically, Young means when he refers to Glaha's engineering background. Glaha may have formally studied engineering during the break in his employment with the Bureau from 1926 to 1930, or Young may have been referring to Glaha's drafting skills.

18. 1931–1936 Boulder Canyon Project-Hoover Dam organization charts; NARA-RMR, RG 115.

19. Letter dated 11/23/31, from Young to Commissioner Mead; NARA-W, RG 115. Some motion picture equipment was also requested, but was denied.

20. Letter dated 12/12/31, from Commissioner Mead to Young; NARA-W, RG 115.

21. Letter dated 11/23/31, from Young to Commissioner Mead; NARA-W, RG 115.

22. Letter dated 1/7/32, from Young to Commissioner Mead; NARA-W, RG 115.

23. Inventory attached to memorandum dated 5/18/36, from Glaha to E. K. Burlew, administrative assistant to the Secretary, Department of the Interior; NARA-W, RG 115.

24. In the absence of a telephoto lens, Glaha learned to be more adaptable, as indicated by the following statement: "I have found that an enlargement made from a section of a negative exposed through a lens of what we call normal focal length is preferable to a contact print from a negative exposed through a so-called telephoto lens which is apt to exhibit a distorted perspective and an erratic spatial readjustment." Ben D. Glaha, "Progress Engineering Photography," in *The Complete Photographer: A Guide to Amateur and Professional Photography*, vol. 8 (New York: National Education Alliance, 1943), 3007.

25. Letter dated 10/24/32 (sent separately from the enlargements), from Young to Commissioner Mead; NARA-W, RG 115.

26. Letter dated 7/27/32, from Norman Gallison, Six Companies, Press and Public Relations Division, to Commissioner Mead; NARA-W, RG 115.

Chapter 3. The Bureau's Use of Glaha's Photographs

1. F. Jack Hurley, in his *Portrait of a Decade: Roy Stryker and the Development of Documentary Photography in the Thirties* (Baton Rouge: Louisiana State University Press, 1972), viii, says, "70% of all federal agencies used pictures in one way or another during the 1930s."

2. Regarding the combination of pictures and text, Maren Stange states in her *Symbols of Ideal Life: Social Documentary Photography in America, 1890–1950* (New York: Cambridge University Press, 1989), xiv, "Not the photograph alone then, but the image set in relation to a written caption, an associated text, and a presenting agency . . . consisted the documentary mode." All of Glaha's images were captioned, placed in some sort of text, lecture, or display, and presented under the rubric of the Bureau.

3. William Stott, *Documentary Expression and Thirties America* (New York: Oxford University Press, 1973), 20.

4. Ulrich Keller, *The Highway as Habitat: A Roy Stryker Documentation, 1943–1955* (Santa Barbara, Calif.: University Art Museum, 1986), 29.

5. Ibid.

6. Betty Houchin Winfield, *FDR and the News Media* (Urbana and Chicago: University of Illinois Press, 1990), 87.

7. Ibid.

8. Ibid, 37.

9. Ickes was in office from 1932 to 1945. Here I refer to Ickes's tenure from 1933 to 1936, the critical years in which the construction of Hoover Dam coincided with the New Deal. Mead was commissioner from 1926 to 1936.

10. Jane D. Ickes, ed., *The Secret Diary of Harold L. Ickes: The First Thousand Days, 1933–1936* (New York: Simon and Schuster, 1953), 444–445. Graham White reiterated FDR's desire to control the release of information and his mandate

that information be released only through official channels: "Roosevelt made strenuous efforts to control the release of unauthorized information. . . . [H]e sought to funnel all information and contacts with the press through departmental press agents; and he lectured department heads on the dangers of discussing with reporters matters relating to other departments or agencies." Graham J. White, *FDR and the Press* (Chicago: University of Chicago Press, 1979), 33.

11. Letter dated 5/6/31, from Commissioner Mead to Mr. E. C. Schmidt, Director of News Service, Union Pacific System; NARA-W, RG 115.

12. Memorandum dated 2/26/32, from Hugh A. Brown, Director, Reclamation Economics, to Commissioner Mead; NARA-W, RG 115.

13. Three individuals who worked with Glaha during his Bureau tenure concurred with the idea that he was allowed to work more or less independently: Wesley Nell, Glaha's nephew and assistant on the Central Valley Project (interviewed by the author 4/28/90); Don Westphal, Glaha's driver in 1944, who later worked in the darkroom, printing from Glaha's negatives (interviewed by the author 5/18/92); and Rupert Spearman, who succeeded Glaha as the photographer at Boulder Dam and met Glaha on some of his return visits to the dam (telephone interview with the author 8/13/92).

14. For a thorough discussion of "shooting scripts," see Keller, *The Highway as Habitat*, 34–35. He differentiates between the "hierarchically rigid procedures at *Life* and *Look*" and FSA photography group supervisor Roy Stryker's methodology; for Stryker, "Although the script provided direction, it was taken for granted that it would grow and change during the work on location." Any directions Glaha received must have been born of a system similar to Stryker's; Glaha apparently was allowed to adjust his shooting on the basis of construction developments he encountered from day to day.

15. Telephone interview with Rupert Spearman, 8/13/92.

16. See letter dated 8/10/36, from Glaha to Acting Commissioner John C. Page; NARA-W, RG 115. Glaha outlines his plans to photograph the most recent construction at the dam site.

17. Letter dated 3/11/32, from Director of Reclamation Economics Brown to Young; NARA-W, RG 115.

18. Letter dated 4/4/32, from Commissioner Mead to Frank T. Crowe, Manager of Construction, Six Companies; NARA-W, RG 115.

19. Several such camera stations were most likely used for the duration of the construction process. One station consisted of a concrete and steel pedestal and was located "at a high point overlooking the dam site." Mounted on that pedestal was a motion picture camera in which a few feet of film were exposed daily in order to make a progressive record of construction on the dam (letter dated 2/12/34, from Young to Commissioner Mead; NARA-W, RG 115). Still images also were probably shot from such manufactured sites, and less permanent settings were certainly employed as well.

20. Joseph E. Stevens, *Hoover Dam: An American Adventure* (Norman: University of Oklahoma Press, 1988), 103. Stevens provides an excellent discussion of the work of the high scalers and the dangers those daring and acrobatic men experienced.

21. Ben Glaha, "Boulder Dam: The Photography of Engineering Works," *U.S. Camera* no. 2 (January–February 1939): 18. Glaha states, "I could tell you stories of . . . working in rigging on the canyon walls."

22. Stevens, *Hoover Dam*, 185.

23. "Scenic Wonderland Opened as Waters Pile Up back of Hoover Dam," *Los Angeles Times* (rotogravure), December 22, 1935, 2. The text accompanying the photographs states, "Some of the subjects shown had never been photographed before."

24. The Six Companies photographer(s) is/are not usually cited by name. A 1931 article lists W. J. (Walter) Lubken as "photographer for Six Companies." See Philip Schuyler, "Hoover Dam Constructionists," *Western Construction News* 6 (December 10, 1931): 635.

25. George Pettitt, *So Boulder Dam Was Built* (Berkeley, Calif.: Lederer, Street and Zeus, 1935). Other texts by Pettitt include *Berkeley: The Town and Gown of It* (Berkeley, Calif.: Howell-North Books, 1973), *Prisoners of Culture* (New York: Scribner's, 1970), and *Twenty-eight Years in the Life of a University President* (Berkeley: University of California Press, 1966).

26. Letter dated 12/24/35, from Young to Commissioner Mead; NARA-W, RG 115.

27. This conclusion is based on the fact that I have yet to locate such an image.

28. Karal Ann Marling, *Wall-to-Wall America: A Cultural History of Post-Office Murals in the Great Depression* (Minneapolis: University of Minnesota Press, 1982), 9.

Chapter 4. Machine Aesthetic

1. Christopher Phillips, "Resurrecting Vision: The New Photography in Europe between the Wars," in *The New Vision: Photography between the World Wars* (New York: Metropolitan Museum of Art, 1989), 65.

2. Thomas P. Hughes, *American Genesis: A Century of Invention and Technological Enthusiasm, 1870–1970* (New York: Viking, 1989), 3.

3. Ibid., 5.

4. Judith Mara Gutman, *Lewis W. Hine: Two Perspectives* (New York: Grossman, 1974), 43.

5. Ibid., 78.

6. Paul Strand, "Photography and the New God," *Broom* 3, no. 4 (1922), reprinted in Nathan Lyons, ed., *Photographers on Photography* (Englewood Cliffs, N.J.: Prentice Hall, 1966), 138.

7. Richard Guy Wilson, *The Machine Age in America, 1918–1941* (New York: Brooklyn Museum/Harry N. Abrams, 1986), 36. For additional discussions of the machine age, see Donald J. Bush, *The Streamlined Decade* (New York: George Braziller, 1975); Siegfried Giedion, *Mechanization Takes Command* (New York: W. W. Norton, 1969); and Museum of Modern Art, *Machine Art* (New York: Museum of Modern Art, 1934).

8. Phillips, "Resurrecting Vision," 73. Phillips does an excellent job of delineating the additional influences of Cubism, Expressionism, futurism, and the Dada movement, which the scope of this text does not allow us to explore. See ibid., 70–77.

9. Ibid., 77, 78.

10. It should be noted here that at this time not all imagists were content to interpret static topics. Phillips, for example, describes the 1911 attempt of brothers Anton and Arturo Bragaglia to convey dynamic motion in still images by making slow exposures of gestures, such as a hand fingering a string instrument. See ibid., 68. A few years later, filmmakers would begin placing cameras on wheels in order to track and close in on actors in motion.

11. Ben Glaha, "Boulder Dam: The Photography of Engineering Works," *U.S. Camera* no. 2 (January–February 1939): 79.

12. For a discussion of Sheeler's participation in the exhibition, see Beaumont Newhall, "Photo Eye of the 1920's: The Deutsche Werkbund Exhibition of 1929," in David Mellor, ed., *Germany: The New Photography, 1927–33* (London: Arts Council of Great Britain, 1978), 83.

13. Wilson, *The Machine Age in America*, 24.

14. Glaha, "Boulder Dam," 18.

15. Karen Lucic, *Charles Sheeler and the Cult of the Machine* (Cambridge, Mass.: Harvard University Press, 1991), 90. In addition to his industrial topic, Sheeler examined "rural, pre-industrial artifacts" (42). Whether Sheeler's duality of imagery was the inspiration for Glaha's "off-site" nonindustrial subjects is not known.

16. Vicki Goldberg, *Margaret Bourke-White: A Biography* (New York: Harper & Row, 1986), 102–103.

17. Ibid., 110.

18. Regarding Margaret Bourke-White's general exclusion of people from her photographs, Goldberg states, "Both Sheeler's work and Bourke-White's celebrate the force and splendid design of technology without paying attention to the worker. . . . Occasionally, Bourke-White's pictures do show workers tending the ladles or ovens or standing about to give scale, pointing up the vastness of technology and the smallness of man, but machines are the true subject." See ibid., 88.

19. Alan Trachtenberg, "Ever-the Human Document" in *America & Lewis Hine: Photographs, 1904–1940* (Millerton, N.Y.: Aperture, 1977), 134. Thomas F. Barrow further indicates Hine's divergence from the artistic practices of his time: "Whenever Hine's work is exhibited or reproduced, one of the more curious aspects is the absence of any evidence that he was influenced by visual phenomena of the time; the work of Man Ray, Andre Breton, Marcel Duchamp; or by his visit to Alfred Stieglitz and An American Place." Quoted in Lewis Wickes Hine, *Reproductions from Original Lewis W. Hine Negatives in the George Eastman House Archive* (Rochester, N.Y.: George Eastman House, 1970), 1.

20. Regarding the decreasing appearance of the human form in art, Barbara Melosh states, "Industrial photography, such as the work of Margaret Bourke-White, often achieved its effects by startling angles and dramatic contrasts in scale that emphasized the frailty of the human form set against looming metal and cement elements. In some cases, photographers touched by modernism eliminated the human entirely to exploit the abstract potential of mass, line, and shadow in the artifacts of industry." Barbara Melosh, *Engendering Culture: Manhood and Womanhood in New Deal Public Art and Theater* (Washington, D.C.: Smithsonian Institution Press, 1991), 121–122.

21. Gutman, *Hine: Two Perspectives*, 27.

22. In defense of those images where Glaha did specifically photograph workers on the project, it is important to acknowledge precedents for worker studies during the period. For example, Judith Gutman found that Lewis Hine's well-publicized series of photographs of the erection of the Empire State Building did manage to find a balance between images of girders rising above New York and the individuals who were responsible for their orchestration into a skyscraper. See ibid., 34. Glaha, who made it a point to be aware of current art and photographic trends, was more than likely aware of Hine's efforts, and some of Glaha's iconographic and heroic images may be traceable to Hine's example. For instance, Glaha's *Rigger on Cableway Headtower during Construction* (before 1935) shares with Hine's *Empire State Building under Construction. On the Mooring Mast, a Quarter of a Mile above the Street* (1930/1931) the heroism of a man precariously perched astride a steel construct, seemingly dwarfed in scale but clearly mandating the situation.

After the research for this book was completed, I was notified by Mark Hayward, Project Manager of the *Imagination to Image* project at the Museum of Science and Industry in Chicago, that the Museum had recently discovered that it has twenty-seven Glaha photographs. The images are from a set of thirty-three that the Bureau of Reclamation donated to the Museum in 1935. The group is composed of several images, each showing a workman at a different task, which I had not previously seen. The existence of the worker portraits and their exhibition may be explained by the fact that the Bureau received Public Works Administration funding for the dam project in 1934, and images of men at work were proof that the funds were being well utilized to provide jobs and to complete a large public works project. Overall, however, the number of images of single (or not more than three) workers constitutes a very small portion of the entire body of Glaha's Hoover Dam photographs.

23. The influence of painting on photography (and vice versa) during this period is a topic worthy of a chapter in itself. It bears mentioning, however, that works of many painters of the period addressed industrial topics, such as Sheeler's *Classic Landscape* (1931) and Charles Demuth's *My Egypt* (1927). Karen Lucic states that it was important for photographers and painters alike to examine industrial topics, not only to solidify one's position as a modernist but also for the express purposes of establishing and solidifying America's identity as a leading industrial nation. See Lucic, *Charles Sheeler*, 34. They did not always, however, convey a positive attitude toward industrialization. In his *Incense of a New Church* (1921), for example, Demuth skeptically regards industry as a secular religion. The contributions of Francis Picabia and Marcel Duchamp also bear mentioning, the former for his selection of machine forms not *in situ* but in isolation, and the latter for the freedom to appropriate objects directly from the environment and declare them works of art. Finally, while Glaha shared none of Diego Rivera's overt political aims, both he and Glaha depicted the utilization of natural resources and the machine's ability to liberate man from nature's domination. A particularly apt example would be Rivera's mural *Detroit Industry* (1932–1933).

24. Glaha's nephew, Wesley Nell, spoke of Glaha's awareness of current art trends. Interview with the author, 4/28/90.

25. Letter dated 12/26/34, from Elwood Mead, Commissioner, Bureau of Reclamation, to Hon. Harold L. Ickes, Secretary of the Interior; NARA-W, RG 115.

26. The volume is in the holdings of the Library of Congress. No other such folios have been located to date, and it is possible that they have been dismantled and their images dispersed among private and public collections. Further evidence that Glaha penned the illustrations is the fact that several of the sketches are based on his photographs.

27. Glaha, "Boulder Dam," 18. Yet Glaha was not without a sense of humor regarding his photographic work and once stated, "However, I once spent three days crawling around between the steel ribs of a huge gate photographing rivet holes. My ideals of photographic integrity and technical purity were at a low ebb at about the three hundredth hole and were practically nil when the job was over." Ibid.

28. Glaha had exhibited prior to January 1935, but no extensive documentation remains from that period. The single pre–January 1935 show for which substantive information remains is a November–December 1933 exhibition at Everything Photographic (an Eastman Kodak store) in Los Angeles. At the Kodak store, Glaha exhibited fifty-three bromide enlargements "of some of the more spectacular and pictorial aspects" of the work at Boulder Dam. Correspondence from Everything Photographic indicates that the exhibition was enthusiastically received by some three hundred attendees. Construction Engineer Walker Young commented, "Such showings have resulted in a wider and more sympathetic general understanding of the work in progress here." See letter dated 12/8/33, from H. S. Wetmore (Sgd.), Eastman Kodak Stores, Everything Photographic, Los Angeles, to B. D. Glaha; NARA-W, RG 115. See also letter dated 1/24/34, from Young to Commissioner Mead; NARA-W, RG 115.

29. For information regarding Dixon, see Ansel Adams, "Maynard Dixon: An Artist, a Friend," *Four Winds: The International Forum for Native American Art, Literature and History* 2 (Winter 1981); Wesley M. Burnside, *Maynard Dixon, Artist of the West* (Provo, Utah: Brigham Young University Press, 1973); and Donald J. Hagerty, *Desert Dreams: The Art and Life of Maynard Dixon* (Layton, Utah: Gibbs Smith, 1993).

30. Quoted in letter dated 5/14/34, from Construction Engineer Young to Commissioner Mead; NARA-W, RG 115.

31. Letter dated 5/15/35, from Young to Commissioner Mead; NARA-W, RG 115. Despite exhaustive research, no further information has been uncovered regarding Adams's lecture.

32. Letter dated 5/14/34, from Young to Commissioner Mead; NARA-W, RG 115.

33. Julia Gethman Andrews, "Artists and Their Work," *San Diego Union*, March 10, 1935. Clipping from the collection of George Rinhart.

34. An article in the *Stockton Daily Evening Record* indicates that the photographs were sent to Stockton "directly from the University of Illinois, where they are now being shown." See Dorothy Hayne, "At the Gallery Museum," *Stockton Daily Evening Record*, home edition, April 20, 1935, 4. Clipping from the Haggin Museum: Pioneer Museum and Haggin Galleries archives. Bureau of Reclamation correspondence makes no mention of an exhibition at the University of Illinois. For example, a letter dated 5/15/35, from Construction Engineer Young to Commissioner Mead, listing the various museums and galleries in which Glaha's work appeared from January to May 1935, does not include the university in the list of venues; NARA-W, RG 115.

35. Dorothy Hayne, "At the Gallery Museum," *Stockton Daily Evening Record*, home edition, May 4, 1935, 16. Clipping from the Haggin Museum Archives.

36. Dorothy Hayne, "At the Gallery Museum," *Stockton Daily Evening Record*, home edition, May 11, 1935, 16. Clipping from the Haggin Museum Archives. Further evidence that Glaha's images were celebrated as artistic works occurred during the exhibition of his Boulder Dam and Grand Coulee Dam images at the Public Library in Milwaukee, September 5 to 27, 1935, and the publication in the *Los Angeles Times* (December 22, 1935) of his images of the landscapes newly accessible via the accumulating waters of the Colorado River behind Hoover Dam. Hence, with the varied exhibition venues, the Bureau accumulated significant publicity regarding its efforts in Black Canyon. The Milwaukee display was announced in *The Reclamation Era* 25 (September 1935): 185. The *Los Angeles Times* images appeared in the rotogravure section, 2.

37. Memorandum dated 5/16/35, from Construction Engineer Young to the Commissioner; NARA-W, RG 115. Glaha's images are still marketed today. Although a 1934 signed gelatin silver print was offered for sale by Christie's, New York, in 1992 and did not sell, a signed 1935 gelatin silver print sold for $25,000 at Sotheby's, New York, in 1993. Both images were from the Hoover Dam construction series.

38. Ibid.

39. Memorandum dated 5/25/35, from Commissioner Mead to Young, Boulder City; NARA-W, RG 115.

40. The National Museum is today referred to as the Smithsonian. Fifty-one photographs were on display "during the month of August." Letter dated 8/6/35, from J. E. Graf, Associate Director, Smithsonian Institution, United States National Museum, to Commissioner Mead; NARA-W, RG 115.

41. Letter dated 7/29/35, from Commissioner Mead to Secretary of the Interior Ickes; NARA-W, RG 115. Also letter dated 8/1/35, from Secretary of the Interior Ickes to the Secretary of State; NARA-W, RG 115.

42. Letter dated 7/29/35, from Commissioner Mead to Hon. Isabella Greenway, House of Representatives; NARA-W, RG 115.

43. After the research for this book was completed, the Museum of Science and Industry in Chicago discovered that it has a holding of twenty-seven Glaha photographs (see n. 22 above). In an October 23, 1935, letter from Elwood Mead, Commissioner of the Bureau of Reclamation, to Trent E. Sanford, Curator of Architecture at the Museum of Science and Industry, Mead said he was sending Sanford some Glaha photographs that "were exhibited in the National Museum in Washington and prompted a great deal of comment." Thus it appears that more than one set of Glaha images was used for

exhibition and distribution. The Ickes portfolio summarizes photographically the processes of the creation of the dam and Boulder City by providing a range of images from panoramas to depictions of how specific construction tasks were completed. The Museum of Science and Industry group contains some of the same images as the Ickes portfolio, but it also includes more worker portraits, which portray the government's active role in increasing employment and completing public works projects. The two sets of images further highlight the aesthetic/documentary duality of Glaha's Hoover Dam photographs. Letter dated 10/23/35, from Mead to Sanford, courtesy of the Museum of Science and Industry.

Chapter 5. Documents for Publicity

1. Pete Daniel and Sally Stein stated, "The larger the federal government grew, the more it depended upon popular graphic forms to convince people that government intervention was beneficial and proper." Pete Daniel and Sally Stein, "Introduction," in Pete Daniel et al., *Official Images: New Deal Photography* (Washington, D.C.: Smithsonian Institution Press, 1987), xi.

2. Letter dated 2/25/31, from R. F. Walter, Chief Engineer, to Elwood Mead, Commissioner of the Bureau of Reclamation; NARA-RMR, RG 115. George O. Gillingham succinctly stated, "The dividing line between 'publicity' and 'propaganda' is hazy in Federal information operations." George O. Gillingham, *Behind Washington's Paper Curtain: An ABC of Government Public Relations* (Philadelphia: Dorrance, 1968), 6.

3. Memorandum dated 9/19/31, from Walker R. Young, Construction Engineer, to Commissioner Mead; NARA-RMR, RG 115.

4. Memorandum dated 11/24/31, from Construction Engineer Young to Commissioner Mead; NARA-W, RG 115.

5. In comparing the photographic documentation of the Bureau and Six Companies, it is interesting to note that the Six Companies images include a greater number of shots of workers at their various tasks than do the Bureau images. The Bureau seems more focused on the dam structure itself, perhaps a result of the desire to eschew references to the risks involved in creating the structure.

6. Order no. 630, dated 5/20/33, from Harold L. Ickes, Secretary of the Interior; NARA-W, RG 115. As an interesting side note, in August 1934 the Bureau was approached by Warner Brothers Pictures regarding a proposed film, portions of which would be shot at the dam site. Upon reviewing an advance copy of the story line, Construction Engineer Young wrote to the studio, indicating several concerns regarding the manner in which the project and its employees were portrayed. For example, the script called for bums loitering and sleeping in the public park, a high scaler performing acrobatic stunts in his bosun's chair, and a gambling hall within Boulder City limits. Young emphasized that each of these scenes was objectionable; it seems that even in the realm of Hollywood make-believe, the Bureau had an image to uphold. See letter dated 8/25/34, from Young to Mr. Joseph J. Barry, Location Department, Warner Bros. and First National Studios; NARA-RMR, RG 115.

7. In one instance, Acting Commissioner Dent went so far as to comment on the manner in which one article proposed to represent the weather in Boulder City: "Mr. Carter has made several references to the prevailing heat at Boulder City, but has made no reference to the fine winter climate." Letter dated 10/18/32, from the Acting Commissioner to Mr. Sims Ely, City Manager, Boulder City, Nev.; NARA-W, RG 115.

8. Letter dated 4/18/32, from the Acting Commissioner to Construction Engineer Young; NARA-W, RG 115.

9. Memorandum dated 11/24/31, from Young to Commissioner Mead; NARA-RMR, RG 115. Also letter dated 12/10/31, from Commissioner Mead to Young; NARA-RMR, RG 115.

10. Letter dated 12/10/31, from Commissioner Mead to Young; NARA-RMR, RG 115.

11. Letter dated 8/30/32, from Commissioner Mead to Chief Engineer Walter; NARA-W, RG 115.

12. See Ulrich Keller, *The Highway as Habitat: A Roy Stryker Documentation, 1943–1955* (Santa Barbara, Calif.: University Art Museum, 1986), 27. Coincident with post-Depression consumer dissatisfaction with business practices, "By 1933, the emergence of the 'public relations council' was noted as a recent and significant development."

13. *New York Times* (November 18, 1934) and *Washington Star*, sec. E (November 25, 1934). The *Star* clipping caption reads, "Night and day, the big job goes ahead at Boulder Dam. Here's a view of the great Colorado River project as the night shift works under floodlights." Photograph clippings, NARA-W, RG 115. Glaha wrote that to achieve this image he made two exposures: one underexposure was made at twilight, and another exposure was superimposed after darkness had fallen. "Progress Engineering Photography," in *The Complete Photographer: A Guide to Amateur and Professional Photography*, vol. 8 (New York: National Educational Alliance, 1943), 3010.

14. *New York Times Magazine*, May 12, 1935, 1; clipping, NARA-W, RG 115. The photograph accompanies an article by Secretary of the Interior Harold L. Ickes, "Public Works for Social Gain." International publicity was demonstrated when other Glaha images supported two articles in a Swiss publication, *Technische Rundschau*. The articles appeared on May 25 and June 1, 1934. *Technische Rundschau* was published in Bern and, as its title indicates, had a technical readership. Commissioner Mead sanctioned the sending of descriptive material, technical data, and photographs to the articles' author, Paul Sidler. See letter dated 6/26/34, from Paul Sidler to Commissioner Mead; NARA-W, RG 115.

15. "Boulder Canyon Project" photographs, for example appear in *The Reclamation Era* 23 (February 1932): 27. Other examples of Glaha photographs are in "Boulder City Firefighters," 23 (March 1932): 64; and "Boulder City Buildings," 23 (March 1932): 67.

16. *The Reclamation Era* 25 (January 1935).

17. Letter dated 6/8/32, from Russell V. Williams, Department Head, Rotary International, to U.S. Department of Agriculture, Reclamation Service Bureau; NARA-W, RG 115. Acting Commissioner's letter to Williams is dated 6/11/32; NARA-W, RG 115.

18. *Boulder Dam Power: A Pictorial History* (San Francisco: Electrical West, 1936), unpaginated.

19. Citation signed by Secretary of the Interior Chapman. Collection of George Rinhart.

20. Willard Van Dyke, "The Work of Ben Glaha," *Camera Craft* 42 (April 1935): 171. Van Dyke was a charter member of Group f64, comprised of photographers Ansel Adams, Imogen Cunningham, John Paul Edwards, Sonya Noskowiak, Henry Swift, and Edward Weston, all of whom believed that an image should have maximum sharpness in both foreground and background. The group's name is based on the camera aperture setting that allows for such detail of exposure. See Leslie Squyres Calmes, *The Letters between Edward Weston and Willard Van Dyke* (Tucson: Center for Creative Photography, University of Arizona, 1992); or Paul Schranz, dir., *Willard Van Dyke* (Cincinnati, Ohio: Images Productions, 1983) (videorecording).

21. "Boulder Canyon Project Notes," *The Reclamation Era* 23 (December 1932): 197; and U.S. Department of the Interior, Bureau of Reclamation, *Annual Project History: Boulder Canyon Project, Hoover Dam* (Washington, D.C.: U.S. Bureau of Reclamation, Washington Office, Engineering Files, 1932), 220. Copy of *Annual Project History*, NARA-W.

22. *Grouting Concrete Lining* also appeared in one of the *Technische Rundschau* articles discussed in note 14.

23. Ben Glaha, "Boulder Dam: The Photography of Engineering Works," *U.S. Camera* no. 2 (January–February 1939): 18.

24. W. H. Buntin, *View-Book of the Boulder (Hoover) Dam* (Los Angeles: Angelus Press, 1933/1940 [?]), Bancroft

Library, University of California, Berkeley; and the Barrett Company, *Boulder Dam: A Modern Engineering Triumph* (New York: Barrett Company, 1936), NARA-W, RG 115.

25. *Boulder Dam: A Modern Engineering Triumph*, unpaginated.

26. It should be noted that the booklet's text acknowledges the contributions of Six Companies and Babcock and Wilcox as well.

27. *Boulder Dam: A Modern Engineering Triumph*, unpaginated.

28. An effort similar to that of the Barrett Company was undertaken by the Ingersoll-Rand Company. Ingersoll-Rand, supplier of air compressors, rock drills, pumps, and other products for the project, throughout the construction process had received favorable publicity about its efforts in *Compressed Air* magazine. Thus Ingersoll-Rand, in conjunction with *Compressed Air* magazine and Six Companies, from time to time reprinted articles from *Compressed Air*. Eventually, the reprinted articles were bound together in a booklet titled *The Story of Hoover Dam* (Las Vegas: Nevada Publications, 1934). The booklet is still being reprinted. The majority of its photographs are Six Companies images, although some Glaha photographs were incorporated as well. While the booklet is much more technical than the Barrett publication, owing to its in-depth articles on many aspects of the construction process, it celebrates the overall effort while simultaneously promoting the vendor, the Bureau, and Six Companies. The Bureau itself also produced a large number of booklets and pamphlets in which carefully created marriages of photographs and printed matter were targeted to meet specific purposes. Some publications, such as the Department of the Interior's booklet *Dams and Control Works: A Description of Representative Storage and Diversion Dams and High-Pressure Reservoir Outlet Works Constructed by the Bureau of Reclamation* (Washington, D.C.: U.S. Government Printing Office, 1938), discussed a variety of projects undertaken by the Bureau. The chapter on Boulder Dam was illustrated by photographs, some of which were Glaha's. *Dams and Control Works* was intended for a readership of engineers, teachers, and students. Commissioner Page stated regarding the booklet: "[O]ur book *Dams and Control Works* has been well received and I believe will reflect credit to the Department and to this Bureau. . . . [I]ssuance of these books provides a means of informing the public concerning the work of the Department and of the Bureau." Memorandum for the Secretary of the Interior by John C. Page, Commissioner, dated 5/17/38; NARA-W, RG 115. Other Bureau publications addressed the Hoover Dam Project alone. *Construction Features at Boulder Dam* was, for example, a very technically oriented publication with articles such as P. A. Kinzie's "Hydraulic Valves and Gates for Boulder Dam: The Design and Fabrication of the Needle Valves and Paradox Emergency Gates." *Construction Features at Boulder Dam* (Washington, D.C.: U.S. Department of the Interior, Bureau of Reclamation, 1934). Glaha's more technical photographs were used to illustrate the text, such as his picture of the recess blasted in the canyon wall to situate the outlet works.

29. Keller, *The Highway as Habitat*, 31.

30. Ibid.

31. Boulder Dam Service Bureau, *Construction of Boulder Dam* (Boulder City, Nev.: Boulder Dam Service Bureau, 1934). The booklet, with some modifications, including a change in its title to *Construction of Hoover Dam*, is currently in its twenty-seventh edition and is published in Las Vegas by KC Publications.

In at least one instance, Bureau materials were also distributed in conjunction with an exhibition of Glaha's salon prints. During an exhibition of his prints at the Museum of Science and Industry in Chicago, the Bureau provided the Museum with at least one handout for distribution to Museum guests. In an October 23, 1935, letter from Elwood Mead, Commissioner of the Bureau of Reclamation, to Trent E. Sanford, Curator of Architecture at the Museum of Science and Industry, Mead states, "Three hundred copies of questions and answers on Boulder Dam are coming to you under separate cover, as requested, for distribution at the exhibit. I regret to advise the leaflet distributed at the Century of Progress Exposition is now out of print. However, we are about to print a new booklet of photographs on Boulder Dam. . . . [I]f it is material you would like to distribute, I can arrange to send you a small supply." Letter dated 10/23/35, from Mead to Sanford, courtesy of the Museum of Science and Industry.

32. Memorandum dated 1/13/36, from Commissioner Mead to the Construction Engineer, Boulder City; NARA-W, RG 115.

33. *Boulder Dam* (Washington, D.C.: Bureau of Reclamation, Department of the Interior, n.d. [ca. 1936?]), located with correspondence dated 1/13/36, from the Commissioner to the Construction Engineer; NARA-W, RG 115.

34. [Boulder City Chamber of Commerce] *Boulder Dam: The World's Most Impressive Engineering Spectacle . . . the Center of an Area of Unsurpassed Scenic and Historical Interest* (n.d. [ca. 1936?]); NARA-W, RG 115. The folder is undated, except for a pencil notation on the cover, "File 9/24/36." It is quite similar in its text, layout, and photographs to an identically titled leaflet located with correspondence dated 5/7/35, from the Assistant to the Commissioner to Mr. P. S. Webb, Boulder City Chamber of Commerce. In her letter to Webb, she states, "You really have something to crow about and I want to congratulate you on the general get-up of the folder." It is, therefore, safe to assume that both folders are Chamber of Commerce publications.

35. The attribution of the map to Glaha is based on "Ben Glaha Chartographer," in the lower right-hand corner. Given Glaha's drafting and artistic background, it is not surprising that he could create such graphics.

36. Joseph E. Stevens, *Hoover Dam: An American Adventure* (Norman: University of Oklahoma Press, 1988), 260.

37. The leaflet indicates that the readings were based on official records kept for a period of three years by the U.S. Department of the Interior's Bureau of Reclamation. It is interesting to note that the 1997 edition of the *California/Nevada Tour Book* of the American Automobile Association states that temperatures range between 25 and 70 degrees Fahrenheit from November through February, climb to warmer levels in March, and reach well over 100 degrees Fahrenheit from June through August. American Automobile Association, *California/Nevada Tour Book* (Heathrow, Fla.: American Automobile Association, 1997), 230.

38. *Boulder Dam* (Washington, D.C.: U.S. Department of the Interior, Bureau of Reclamation, n.d. [ca. 1939?]). Located with correspondence dated 1/16/39; NARA-W, RG 115.

39. Ibid., unpaginated. The sentence appears under the heading "Achievements," inside the front cover.

40. Glaha's Hoover Dam images were used in subsequent Bureau publications regarding the dam, for example, *The Story of Boulder Dam*, Conservation Bulletin no. 9 (Washington, D.C.: U.S. Government Printing Office, 1941); NARA-W, RG 115. Other publications, which although broader in scope, included some reference to the dam and incorporated Glaha photographs, too. Examples are the Bureau pamphlet *Federal Reclamation Projects* (Washington, D.C.: U.S. Government Printing Office, 1935) and the Public Works Administration's booklet *PWA: The First 3 Years* (Washington, D.C.: U.S. Government Printing Office, 1936).

41. Ralph B. Simmons, *Boulder Dam and the Great Southwest* (Los Angeles: Pacific Publishers, 1936), title page.

42. Stevens, *Hoover Dam*.

43. Stevens described the extreme working conditions the men faced in writing rather than in photographs. As discussed later in the chapter, no Glaha photographs illustrating negative conditions on the job site or in Boulder City have been located.

44. Harold L. Ickes, *Back to Work: The Story of PWA* (New York: Macmillan, 1935).

45. Carl W. Condit, *American Building Art: The Twentieth Century* (New York: Oxford University Press, 1961).

46. Unfortunately, the extant documents regarding the illustrated lectures, exhibition prints, and transparencies do not always give an attribution of authorship. There are, though, some indicators that Glaha photographs were used to make slides and exhibition enlargements, and those indicators will be discussed.

47. Letter dated 11/4/31, from Commissioner Mead to Chief Engineer Walter; NARA-W, RG 115.

48. Memorandum dated 4/1/32, from Chief Engineer Walter to the Commissioner; NARA-W, RG 115.

49. Letter dated 2/24/34, from Commissioner Mead to Charles B. Stafford, Executive Manager, Department of Commerce and Industry, Cheyenne, Wyoming; NARA-W, RG 115.

50. Agencies independent of the Bureau of Reclamation also created slides from photographs obtained with the Bureau's permission. The American Society of Civil Engineers, for example, requested from the Bureau twenty-three specific photographs. The photographs were made into slides in preparation for a lecture given by Construction Engineer Walker R. Young to the Los Angeles chapter of the organization. Memorandum dated 11/28/32, from Young to the Commissioner; NARA-W, RG 115. Ohio State University also made slides from Bureau photographs. After touring the dam site and examining the on-site photographic records, Ohio State's Dean of the College of Engineering, E. A. Hitchcock, submitted a list of specific Bureau images he desired for the purpose of making lantern slides. Dean Hitchcock planned to utilize the slides in lectures to his students. See letter dated 3/21/34, from E. A. Hitchcock, Dean, College of Engineering, Ohio State University, to Commissioner Mead; NARA-W, RG 115.

51. Letter dated 5/21/32 with document attached, from the Hon. C. Bascom Slemp, Commission of the United States of America, the International Colonial and Overseas Exposition at Paris, to Commissioner Mead; NARA-W, RG 115. See also letter dated 5/27/32, from Commissioner Mead to the Hon. C. Bascom Slemp; NARA-W, RG 115. The latter indicates that the exhibit was "so much admired" that the director of L'Ecole Coloniale requested that it be retained in Paris.

52. Department of the Interior memorandum for the press, dated 6/20/35; NARA-W, RG 115. Also letter dated 3/14/36, from Edith Bennett, Department Representative, Department of the Interior, Office of the Secretary, to Miss M. A. Schnurr, Assistant to the Commissioner, Bureau of Reclamation; NARA-W, RG 115.

53. Memorandum dated 3/23/39, from Walker R. Young, Supervising Engineer, to the Commissioner (with memorandum from Phil Dickinson, Assistant Director of Information, Bureau of Reclamation attached); NARA-W, RG 115.

54. Letter dated 3/3/36, from Chas. L. Wilson, Secretary-Manager, Sixth District Agricultural Association, California State Exposition Building, to John C. Page, Acting Commissioner, U.S. Reclamation Service; NARA-W, RG 115.

55. Letter dated 10/8/35, from the Acting Commissioner to Trent E. Sanford, Curator of Architecture, Museum of Science and Industry, Jackson Park, Chicago; NARA-W, RG 115.

56. Letter dated 10/14/35, from R. C. MacLellan, Advertising Agent, Baltimore and Ohio Railroad, to Commissioner Mead; NARA-W, RG 115.

57. Letter dated 11/11/44, from H. W. Bashore, Commissioner, Bureau of Reclamation, to "Dear Sir"; NARA-W, RG 115. (A handwritten notation on the letter states, "Form letter sent 12–26–44.")

58. In 1931, Construction Engineer Walker Young conducted an inspection of the men's living and working conditions and reported his findings to the commissioner. Young's inspection and report indicate a concern at the Bureau with the manner in which the program was portrayed publicly. In his report, dated December 1931, Young found no serious problems with the method of employment, housing facilities, mess houses, commissary, working conditions, provisions for first aid and hospitalization, and attention to safety measures. He did find "inadequate recreational and educational advantages and . . . no

extensive program is planned by Six Companies." He also suggested that deductions from the wages of employees for quarters, subsistence, and hospitalization services had covered the camp investment and therefore could be reduced in a show of goodwill. Memorandum dated 1/8/31, from Construction Engineer Young to the Commissioner; NARA-RMR, RG 115. Obviously, the dates of the report and of the memorandum are not in chronological sequence. Perhaps Young began 1932 forgetting to write the correct year. An interesting counterpoint to Young's report is a letter from Andy Evans, a waiter employed in the Anderson Brothers Boarding Supply Company dining rooms and kitchens. Evans alleged, "The Chef . . . was observed to be intoxicated at least half the time," and "Some of the food served was not in good condition and on several occasions made some of the men ill." See letter dated 7/23/31, from Andy D. Evans to To Whom it may Concern; NARA-RMR, RG 115. In his findings regarding the Anderson Brothers' mess houses, Young noted that the employees were neat in appearance and were given physical exams twice monthly, and that "No criticism of consequence was heard concerning the food or service." See memorandum dated 1/8/31, cited above.

59. Stevens, *Hoover Dam*, 70–71.

60. Elton Garrett, "Boulder City Is No Longer Man's Town: Family Life Comes to Stay at Government Community at Dam Site," *Las Vegas Evening Review Journal*, September 17, 1931; clipping, NARA-W, RG 115. The article does not indicate by whom, if anyone, Garrett was employed.

61. Claude Rader, "Us Old Boys on Boulder Dam," *Las Vegas Evening Review Journal*, November 9, 1931; clipping, NARA-W, RG 115.

62. Arthur Moore, "Workers Say Boulder Dam Job Is Unsafe," *Rocky Mountain News* [Denver], January 5, 1932; and "Few Accidents Take Lives of Dam Workers," *Rocky Mountain News*, January 6, 1932; both clippings, NARA-W, RG 115.

63. Commissioner Mead, in correspondence with an individual who had visited the dam site and Boulder City and expressed praise regarding both, responded: "The fact that we have gone through three years without any serious labor troubles and with no outbreaks of disease, is more largely due to taking our living accommodations out of the canyon . . . than most people realize." The commissioner's comments indicate a Bureau position that simply does not acknowledge any disturbances. Letter dated 3/26/34, from Commissioner Mead to E. A. Hitchcock, Dean, College of Engineering, Ohio State University; NARA-W, RG 115.

64. George Gillingham offers a more pragmatic reason for the Bureau's lack of response: "the Government is slower in replying to attack in public print. The publicity man for a private concern does not have to go through so much coordination. He usually has a ready and snappy statement to make the headlines. On the other hand, the Federal information man must get many clearances and the resultant release is often a composite of stilted wordage, too belated for press use and too long for popular digest." Gillingham, *Behind Washington's Paper Curtain*, 40. Taking a different, more social-psychological approach, Karal Ann Marling also examined the period's avoidance of portrayals of conflict. Her research addressed government-commissioned post-office murals, although her findings resonate with other government-sponsored projects of the time: "Indeed, the best-loved work murals scrupulously avoided any suggestion of drama, tragic or otherwise, and illustrated with deadpan earnestness the mundane rituals of making a living as a steel-puddler or a cheese-tester. In a sense, by excising abnormalities from factories and mines and by stressing the absolute, unheroic ordinariness of productive labor, work murals became talismanic objects or fetishes. They gave tangible form to hopes for a future in which going to work would be the most routine of human activities." Karal Ann Marling, *Wall-to-Wall America: A Cultural History of Post-Office Murals in the Great Depression* (Minneapolis: University of Minnesota Press, 1982), 19.

65. Margaret Leslie Davis, "The Tide of Doom," *USC Trojan Family Magazine* 25 (Autumn 1993): 29. The events

that occurred during the dam's collapse are excerpted from Davis's biography of Mulholland, *Rivers in the Desert: William Mulholland and the Inventing of Los Angeles* (New York: HarperCollins, 1993).

66. Letter dated 11/25/30, Construction Engineer Young to Chief Engineer Walter; NARA-RMR, RG 115.

67. Ibid.

68. Ibid.

69. Letter dated 3/27/31, from Jos. M. Dixon, First Assistant Secretary, U.S. Department of the Interior, Office of the Secretary, to Mr. Fred Beckert; NARA-RMR, RG 115.

70. Letter dated 7/4/31, from Walter W. Hamilton, C. W. Waner, and John B. Britton to Herbert Hoover, President of the United States; NARA-RMR, RG 115.

71. Letter dated 7/9/31, from Acting Commissioner Dent to Walter W. Hamilton; NARA-RMR, RG 115.

72. Letter dated 7/27/31, from John C. Page, Acting Construction Engineer, to the Commissioner; NARA-RMR, RG 115.

73. Letter dated 5/12/33, from Roy Wilkins, Assistant Secretary, National Association for the Advancement of Colored People, to Hon. Harold L. Ickes, Secretary, Department of the Interior; NARA-RMR, RG 115.

74. Memorandum for the Secretary, dated 5/16/33, from Commissioner Mead; NARA-RMR, RG 115.

75. Nicholas Natanson offers his analysis of how and why African Americans were photographed at work on government projects. He states, "On the government photography front, project shots—designed to justify the use of funds that many New Deal critics did not want spent on poor people in general and blacks in particular—dominated the principal photo-files of the . . . Public Works Administration . . . and related 1930s–40s agencies. Dedication and discipline served as the thematic keynotes for black subjects." *The Black Image in the New Deal: The Politics of FSA Photography* (Knoxville: University of Tennessee Press, 1992), 34.

Chapter 6. Glaha's Contribution Spreads Beyond the Dam

1. Letter dated 6/13/36, from Ben Glaha to John C. Page, Acting Commissioner; National Archives, Washington, D.C., Record Group 115.

2. Ibid.

3. Memorandum dated 6/23/36, from Acting Commissioner Page to E. K. Berlew, Administrative Assistant to the Secretary, Bureau of Reclamation; NARA-W, RG 115.

4. Collection of George Rinhart.

5. Collection of George Rinhart. Bourke-White had photographed the dam in Dnieprostroi, Russia, in 1930, which may have heightened her interest in visiting Hoover Dam.

6. Vicki Goldberg, *Margaret Bourke-White: A Biography* (New York: Harper & Row, 1986), 129. Bourke-White discusses her career in her autobiography, *Portrait of Myself* (New York: Simon and Schuster, 1963). See also Beatrice Siegel, *An Eye on the World: Margaret Bourke-White, Photographer* (New York: F. Warne, 1980).

7. Letter dated 5/14/34, from Construction Engineer Young to Commissioner Mead; NARA-W, RG 115.

8. Examples of William Woollett's work appear in his book *California's Golden Age: With Illustrations and Text* (Santa Barbara, Calif.: Capra Press, 1989).

9. Artist file, National Museum of American Art, Washington, D.C.

10. Woollett's sons, who have graciously granted me permission to reproduce their father's work, do not agree with my conclusions.

11. Memorandum dated 10/10/33, from Construction Engineer Young to the Commissioner; NARA-W, RG 115. The memorandum includes a list of numbers for pictures requested by Woollett. Woollett wrote of his awareness of Glaha's photographs in his text *California's Golden Age*: "The drama of Hoover played continuously day and night between 1931 and 1935, and I followed the news from afar, studying the *Los Angeles Times* sketches of Mr. Owens and the pictures made by the government photographer, Mr. Glaha." See Woollett, *California's Golden Age*, 84.

12. Memorandum dated 10/10/33, from Young to the Commissioner; NARA-W, RG.

13. See memorandum dated 9/17/32, from Young to the Commissioner; NARA-W, RG 115. Per a memorandum dated 10/10/33, from Young to the Commissioner (NARA-W, RG 115), Woollett was not charged for the photographs he requested.

14. The lithograph was one of a group of thirty-nine exhibited at the U.S. National Museum, February 14–28, 1935. The photograph appears in the Ickes portfolio, which was prepared between August and December 1934.

15. The image appeared in the 1935 U.S. National Museum exhibition.

16. The lithograph appeared in the 1935 U.S. National Museum exhibition.

17. The photograph appears in the Ickes portfolio.

18. The folio of images is stored at the National Archives in Washington.

19. An interesting aside is that both artists cited their musical training as an influence on their photography. For example, both men used metronomes in the darkroom to time their printing. See, for example, Ben Glaha, "Boulder Dam: The Photography of Engineering Works," *U.S. Camera* no. 2 (January–February 1939): 18.

Chapter 7. Contemporary Photography

1. Richard Guy Wilson, "The Machine in the Landscape," in his *The Machine Age in America, 1918–1941* (New York: Brooklyn Museum and Harry N. Abrams, 1986), 91.

2. Melissa Healy, "Are West's Dams Set in Stone?" *Los Angeles Times*, March 31, 1994, A1.

3. Ibid, A28.

4. Eric Brazil, "Cooler Runnings," *San Francisco Examiner*, June 2, 1996, A-1, A9.

5. Robert H. Webb, *Grand Canyon, A Century of Change: Rephotography of the 1889–1890 Stanton Expedition* (Tucson: University of Arizona Press, 1996), 209.

6. Robert Adams, *The New West: Landscapes along the Colorado Front Range* (Boulder: Colorado Associated University Press, 1974), v.

7. Ibid.

8. For this insight I am indebted to Drs. Hugo Loaiciga and Richard Church and their University of California at Santa Barbara geography course, "Water in the West" (Winter 1992).

9. Joseph Finkhouse and Mark Crawford, eds., *A River Too Far: The Past and Future of the Arid West* (Reno: Nevada Humanities Committee, 1991), 11.

10. Patricia Nelson Limerick, "The Significance of Deserts in American History from *Desert Passages*," in ibid., 23.

11. Ibid, 19.

12. John McPhee, "A River from *Encounters with the Archdruid*," in *A River Too Far*, 140, 135.

BIBLIOGRAPHY

Adams, Ansel. "Maynard Dixon: An Artist, a Friend." *Four Winds: The International Forum for Native American Art, Literature and History* 2 (Winter 1981).

———. "Photographs of National Parks by Ansel Adams, 1933–42." Washington, D.C.: National Archives and Records Administration. (Folio).

Adams, Robert. *The New West: Photographs along the Colorado Front Range*. Boulder: Colorado Associated University Press, 1974.

Allen, Marion V. *Hoover Dam and Boulder City*. Redding, Calif.: C. P. Printing & Publishing, 1985.

American Automobile Association. *California/Nevada Tour Book*. Heathrow, Fla.: American Automobile Association, 1993.

Andrews, Julia Gethman. "Artists and Their Work." *San Diego Union*, March 10, 1935.

Barrett Company. *Boulder Dam: A Modern Engineering Triumph*. New York: Barrett Company, 1936.

Bauer, Helen. *Water: Riches or Ruin*. Garden City, N.Y.: Doubleday, 1959.

Berkman, Richard L., and W. Kip Viscusi. *Ralph Nader's Study Group Report on the Bureau of Reclamation: Damming the West*. New York: Grossman, 1973.

Betsky, Aaron. "Measured Immensity: Hoover Dam at Fifty." *Progressive Architecture* 66 (September 1985): 38.

"Boulder Canyon Project." *Reclamation Era* 23 (February 1932): 27.

"Boulder Canyon Project Notes." *Reclamation Era* 23 (January 1932): 12, 13.

"Boulder Canyon Project Notes." *Reclamation Era* 23 (December 1932): 197.

[Boulder City Chamber of Commerce]. *Boulder Dam: The World's Most Impressive Engineering Spectacle . . . the Center of an Area of Unsurpassed Scenic and Historical Interest*. 1935 edition. (Leaflet).

Boulder Dam. Washington, D.C.: Bureau of Reclamation, U.S. Department of the Interior, n.d. (ca. 1936?). (Leaflet).

Boulder Dam. Washington, D.C.: Bureau of Reclamation, U.S. Department of the Interior, n.d. (ca. 1939?). (Leaflet).

Boulder Dam Power: A Pictorial History. San Francisco: Electrical West; Boulder City, Nev.: Boulder Dam Service Bureau, 1936.

Boulder Dam Service Bureau. *Construction of Boulder Dam*. Boulder City, Nev.: Boulder Dam Service Bureau, 1934. (Title has been changed to *Construction of Hoover Dam*.)

Bourke-White, Margaret. *Portrait of Myself*. New York: Simon and Schuster, 1963.

Boyle, Robert H. *The Water Hustlers*. San Francisco: Sierra Club, 1971.

Brazil, Eric. "Cooler Runnings." *San Francisco Examiner*, June 2, 1996, A1, A9.

Brookings Institution, Institute for Government Research. *The U.S. Reclamation Service: Its History, Activities and Organization*. New York: D. Appleton, 1919.

Buntin, W. H. *View-Book of the Boulder (Hoover) Dam*. Los Angeles: Angelus Press, 1933/1940(?).

Burnside, Wesley M. *Maynard Dixon, Artist of the West*. Provo, Utah: Brigham Young University Press, 1973.

Bush, Donald J. *The Streamlined Decade*. New York: George Braziller, 1975.

Calmes, Leslie Squyres. *The Letters between Edward Weston and Willard Van Dyke*. Tucson: Center for Creative Photography, University of Arizona, 1992.

Condit, Carl W. *American Building Art: The Twentieth Century*. New York: Oxford University Press, 1961.

Construction of Hoover Dam. Boulder City, Nev.: Boulder Dam Visitors' Bureau, 1950.

Cullen, Allan H. *Rivers in Harness: The Story of Dams*. Philadelphia: Chilton Books, 1962.

Curtis, James. *Mind's Eye, Mind's Truth: FSA Photography Reconsidered*. Philadelphia: Temple University Press, 1989.

Daniel, Pete, et al. *Official Images: New Deal Photography*. Washington, D.C.: Smithsonian Institution Press, 1987.

Davis, Arthur P. "Reclamation of Arid West by Federal Government." *Annals of the American Academy of Political and Social Science* 31 (January 1908): 203—218.

Davis, Margaret Leslie. *Rivers in the Desert: William Mulholland and the Inventing of Los Angeles*. New York: HarperCollins, 1993.

————. "The Tide of Doom." *USC Trojan Family Magazine* 25 (Autumn 1993): 26—35.

Dawdy, Doris Ostrander. *Congress in Its Wisdom: The Bureau of Reclamation and the Public Interest*. Boulder, Colo.: Westview Press, 1989.

D'Harnoncourt, Anne, and Kynaston McShine, eds. *Marcel Duchamp*. New York: Museum of Modern Art, 1973.

Draper, William R. "Irrigation: How the Federal Government Is Reclaiming Arid Land and Almost Giving It Away to the Homeless Man." *Independent* 64 (May 1908): 1172–1178.

Electrical West. *Boulder Dam Power: A Pictorial History*. San Francisco: Electrical West, 1936.

"Engineers-Contractors Committee Finds Hoover Dam Conditions Satisfactory." *Reclamation Era* 23 (February 1932): 32.

Farnham, Emily. *Charles Demuth: Behind a Laughing Mask*. Norman: University of Oklahoma Press, 1971.

Finkhouse, Joseph, and Mark Crawford, eds. *A River Too Far: The Past and Future of the Arid West*. Reno: Nevada Humanities Committee, 1991.

Florman, Samuel C. "Hoover Dam: An American Adventure." *New York Times Book Review*, February 12, 1989, 23.

Garrett, Elton. "Boulder City Is No Longer Man's Town: Family Life Comes to Stay at Government Community at Dam Site." *Las Vegas Evening Review Journal*, September 17, 1931.

Giedion, Siegfried. *Mechanization Takes Command*. New York: W. W. Norton, 1969.

Gillingham, George O. *Behind Washington's Paper Curtain: An ABC of Government Public Relations*. Philadelphia: Dorrance, 1968.

Glaha, Ben. "Boulder City Boasts a Band." *Reclamation Era* 23 (September 1932): 155.

————. "Boulder Dam: The Photography of Engineering Works." *U.S. Camera* no. 2 (January–February 1939): 18–32, 78—79.

————. "Colorado River Resents Being Harnessed." *Reclamation Era* 23 (October 1932): 169.

————. "Development of Boulder City as a Social Unit." *Reclamation Era* 23 (December 1932): 200.

————. "The People Who Have Gone Away." *Reclamation Era* 32 (March 1942): 51–53.

————. "Progress Engineering Photography." In Willard D. Morgan, ed., *The Complete Photographer: A Guide to Amateur and Professional Photography*. Vol. 8, 3006–3015. New York: National Educational Alliance, 1943.

Goin, Peter, ed. *Arid Waters: Photographs from the Water in the West Project*. Reno: University of Nevada Press, 1992.

Goldberg, Vicki. *Margaret Bourke-White: A Biography*. New York: Harper & Row, 1986.

Gutman, Judith Mara. *Lewis W. Hine and the American Social Conscience*. New York: Walker, 1967.

———. *Lewis W. Hine: Two Perspectives*. New York: Grossman, 1974.

Hagerty, Donald J. *Desert Dreams: The Art and Life of Maynard Dixon*. Layton, Utah: Gibbs Smith, 1993.

Hastings, James Rodney, and Raymond M. Turner. *The Changing Mile: An Ecological Study of Vegetation Change with Time in the Lower Mile of an Arid and Semiarid Region*. Tucson: University of Arizona Press, 1965.

Hayne, Dorothy. "At the Gallery Museum." *Stockton Daily Evening Record*, home ed., April 20, 1935, 4.

———. "At the Gallery Museum." *Stockton Daily Evening Record*, home ed., May 4, 1935, 16.

———. "At the Gallery Museum." *Stockton Daily Evening Record*, home ed., May 11, 1935, 16.

Healy, Melissa. "Are West's Dams Set in Stone?" *Los Angeles Times*, March 31, 1994, A1, A28–29.

Hine, Lewis. *Men at Work*. New York: Dover, 1977.

———. *Reproductions from Original Lewis W. Hine Negatives in the George Eastman House Archive*. Rochester, N.Y.: George Eastman House, 1970.

Historical Information on Bureau of Reclamation Hydroelectric Facilities, 1902–1962. Denver: Bureau of Reclamation, 1990.

Holt, L. M. "How the Reclamation Service Is Robbing the Settler." *Overland Monthly and Out West Magazine* 50 (November 1907): 510–512.

———. "Reclamation Service and the Imperial Valley." *Overland Monthly and Out West Magazine* 51 (January 1908): 70–75.

Hughes, Thomas P. *American Genesis: A Century of Invention and Technological Enthusiasm, 1870–1970*. New York: Viking, 1989.

Hunt, Edward Eyre, ed. *The Power Industry and the Public Interest: A Summary of the Results of a Survey of the Relations between the Government and the Electric Power Industry*. New York: Twentieth Century Fund, 1944.

Hurley, F. Jack. *Portrait of a Decade: Roy Stryker and the Development of Documentary Photography in the Thirties*. Baton Rouge: Louisiana State University Press, 1972.

Huth, Hans. *Nature and the American: Three Centuries of Changing Attitudes*. Berkeley and Los Angeles: University of California Press, 1957.

Ickes, Harold L. *America's House of Lords: An Inquiry into the Freedom of the Press*. New York: Harcourt Brace, 1939.

———. *Back to Work: The Story of PWA*. New York: Macmillan, 1935.

———. "Public Works for Social Gain." *New York Times Magazine*, May 12, 1935, 1.

Ickes, Jane D., ed. *The Secret Diary of Harold L. Ickes: The First Thousand Days, 1933–1936*. New York: Simon and Schuster, 1953.

Ingersoll-Rand Company. *The Story of Hoover Dam*. New York: Ingersoll-Rand, 1934.

Jackson, Donald C. *Great American Bridges and Dams*. Washington, D.C.: Preservation Press, 1988.

Jussim, Estelle, and Elizabeth Lindquist-Cook. *Landscape as Photograph*. New Haven: Yale University Press, 1985.

Kaplan, Daile, ed. *Photo Story: Selected Letters and Photographs of Lewis W. Hine*. Washington, D.C.: Smithsonian Institution Press, 1992.

Keller, Ulrich. *The Building of the Panama Canal in Historic Photographs*. New York: Dover, 1983.

———. *The Highway as Habitat: A Roy Stryker Documentation, 1943–1955*. Santa Barbara, Calif.: University Art Museum, 1986.

King, Clarence. *The Helmet of Mambrino*. New York: G. P. Putnam's Sons, 1904.

Kleinsorge, Paul L. *The Boulder Canyon Project: Historical and Economic Aspects*. Stanford, Calif.: Stanford University Press, 1941.

Klett, Mark. *Second View: The Rephotographic Survey Project.* Albuquerque: University of New Mexico Press, 1984.

Kuenzli, Rudolf, and Francis M. Naumann, eds. *Marcel Duchamp: Artist of the Century.* Cambridge, Mass.: MIT Press, 1990.

Lee, Lawrence B. *Reclaiming the American West: An Historiography and Guide.* Santa Barbara, Calif.: American Bibliographical Center–Clio Press, 1980.

Lemenager, Henri V. "The Government's Great Storage Dams: What They Will Accomplish toward the Conservation and Development of the Natural Resources of the West." *Review of Reviews* 37 (June 1908): 689–698.

Limerick, Patricia Nelson. "The Significance of Deserts in American History from *Desert Passages.*" In Joseph Finkhouse and Mark Crawford, eds., *A River Too Far: The Past and Future of the Arid West.* Reno: Nevada Humanities Committee, 1991.

Lucic, Karen. *Charles Sheeler and the Cult of the Machine.* Cambridge, Mass.: Harvard University Press, 1991.

Marling, Karal Ann. *Wall-to-Wall America: A Cultural History of Post-Office Murals in the Great Depression.* Minneapolis: University of Minnesota Press, 1982.

McCamy, James L. *Government Publicity: Its Practice in Federal Administration.* Chicago: University of Chicago Press, 1939.

McCracken, Robert D. *Las Vegas: The Great American Playground.* Fort Collins, Colo.: Marion Street, 1996.

McGaffey, E. "Power, Irrigation and Beauty." *National Republic* 21 (April 1934): 6–7.

Mead, Elwood. "Hoover Dam, World's Largest Irrigation Project." *Architect and Engineer* 105 (June 1931): 69–73.

Mellor, David, ed. *Germany: The New Photography, 1927–33.* London: Arts Council of Great Britain, 1978.

Melosh, Barbara. *Engendering Culture: Manhood and Womanhood in New Deal Public Art and Theater.* Washington, D.C.: Smithsonian Institution Press, 1991.

Moeller, Beverley Bowen. *Phil Swing and Boulder Dam.* Berkeley: University of California Press, 1971.

Moore, Arthur. "Few Accidents Take Lives of Dam Workers." *Rocky Mountain News* (Denver), January 6, 1932.

——. "Workers Say Boulder Dam Job Is Unsafe." *Rocky Mountain News* (Denver), January 5, 1932.

Museum of Modern Art. *Machine Art.* New York: Museum of Modern Art, 1934.

Natanson, Nicholas. *The Black Image in the New Deal: The Politics of FSA Photography.* Knoxville: University of Tennessee Press, 1992.

Nathanson, Milton N. *Updating the Hoover Dam Documents.* [Denver ?]: Bureau of Reclamation, U.S. Department of the Interior, 1978.

Nevada Publications. *The Story of the Hoover Dam.* Las Vegas: Nevada Publications, 1979.

Newhall, Beaumont. "Photo Eye of the 1920's: The Deutsche Werkbund Exhibition of 1929." In David Mellor, ed., *Germany: The New Photography, 1927–33.* London: Arts Council of Great Britain, 1978.

Pettitt, George. *Berkeley: The Town and Gown of It.* Berkeley, Calif.: Howell-North Books, 1973.

——. *Prisoners of Culture.* New York: Scribner's, 1970.

——. *So Boulder Dam Was Built.* Berkeley, Calif.: Lederer, Street and Zeus, 1935.

——. *Twenty-eight Years in the Life of a University President.* Berkeley: University of California Press, 1966.

Phillips, Christopher. "Resurrecting Vision: The New Photography in Europe between the Wars." In *The New Vision: Photography between the World Wars.* New York: Metropolitan Museum of Art, 1989.

Plowden, David. *The Hand of Man on America.* Washington, D.C.: Smithsonian Institution Press, 1971.

Portland Cement Association. *Dams of the World.* Chicago: The Association, 1962.

The Professor Goes West: Illinois Wesleyan University Reports of Major John Wesley Powell's Explorations, 1867–1874. Bloomington: Illinois Wesleyan University Press, 1954.

Public Works Administration. *America Builds: The Record of PWA.* Washington, D.C.: U.S. Government Printing Office, 1939.

———. *PWA: The First Three Years*. Washington, D.C.: U.S. Government Printing Office, 1936.

Rader, Claude. "Us Old Boys on Boulder Dam." *Las Vegas Evening Review Journal*, November 9, 1931.

"Reclamation's New Plans." *Outlook* 89 (May 2, 1908): 5–6.

Richter, Hans. *Dada: Art and Anti-Art*. New York: McGraw-Hill, 1965.

Rivera, Diego. *My Art, My Life*. New York: Citadel Press, 1960.

Robinson, Michael C. *Water for the West: The Bureau of Reclamation, 1902–1977*. Chicago: Public Works Historical Society, 1979.

Rosenblum, Walter, and Naomi Rosenblum, with Alan Trachtenberg. *America & Lewis Hine: Photographs, 1904–1940*. Millerton, N.Y.: Aperture, 1977.

Salander-O'Reilly Galleries. *Morton Livingston Schamberg: The Machine Pastels*. New York: Salander-O'Reilly Galleries, 1986.

Salt, Harriet. *Mighty Engineering Feats*. Freeport, N.Y.: Books for Libraries Press, 1969.

"Scenic Wonderland Opened as Waters Pile Up back of Hoover Dam." *Los Angeles Times Sunday Magazine* (rotogravure), December 22, 1935, 2.

Schranz, Paul, dir. "Willard Van Dyke." Cincinnati: Images Productions, 1983. Videorecording.

Schuyler, Philip. "Hoover Dam Constructionists." *Western Construction News* 6 (December 10, 1931): 632–638.

Schwarz, Jordan A. *The New Dealers: Power Politics in the Age of Roosevelt*. New York: Alfred A. Knopf, 1993.

Shaw, Louise E. *A Century of American Landscape Photography*. Atlanta: High Museum of Art, 1981.

Sheeler, Charles. "Power." *Fortune* 22 (December 1940): 73–84.

Siegel, Beatrice. *An Eye on the World: Margaret Bourke-White, Photographer*. New York: F. Warne, 1980.

Simmons, Ralph B. *Boulder Dam and the Great Southwest*. Los Angeles: Pacific Publishers, 1936.

Stange, Maren. *Symbols of Ideal Life: Social Documentary Photography in America, 1890–1950*. New York: Cambridge University Press, 1989.

Stebbins, Theodore E., Jr., and Norman Keyes, Jr. *Charles Sheeler: The Photographs*. Boston: Museum of Fine Arts, 1987.

Stevens, Joseph E. *Hoover Dam: An American Adventure*. Norman: University of Oklahoma Press, 1988.

The Story of Hoover Dam. Las Vegas: Nevada Publications, 1934.

Stott, William. *Documentary Expression and Thirties America*. New York: Oxford University Press, 1973.

Strand, Paul. "Photography and the New God." Reprinted in Nathan Lyons, ed., *Photographers on Photography*. Englewood Cliffs, N.J.: Prentice Hall, 1966.

Stryker, Roy E., and Paul H. Johnstone. "Documentary Photographs." In *The Cultural Approach to History*. New York: Columbia University Press, 1940.

Szarkowski, John. *The Photographer and the American Landscape*. New York: Museum of Modern Art, 1963.

Tashjian, Dickran. *Skyscraper Primitives: Dada and the American Avant-Garde, 1910–1925*. Middletown, Conn.: Wesleyan University Press, 1975.

Thornton, Gene. *Landscape Photography*. New York: American Photographic Book Publishing, 1984.

Trachtenberg, Alan. *The American Image: Photographs from the National Archives, 1860–1960*. New York: Pantheon Books, 1979.

U.S. Department of the Interior, Bureau of Reclamation. *Annual Project History. Boulder Canyon Project: Hoover Dam*. Washington, D.C.: Bureau of Reclamation, 1932.

———. *Dams and Control Works: A Description of Representative Storage and Diversion Dams and High-Pressure Reservoir Outlet Works Constructed by the Bureau of Reclamation*. Washington, D.C.: U.S. Government Printing Office, 1938.

———. *Federal Reclamation Projects*. Washington, D.C.: U.S. Government Printing Office, 1935.

———. *Historical Information on Bureau of Reclamation Hydroelectric Facilities, 1902–1962*. Denver: Bureau of Reclamation, 1990.

———. *Hoover Dam*. Washington, D.C.: U.S. Government Printing Office, 1985.

———. "Hydraulic Valves and Gates for Boulder Dam. Part III: The Design and Fabrication of Needle Valves and Paradox Emergency Gates." In *Construction Features at Boulder Dam*. Washington, D.C.: Bureau of Reclamation, 1934.

———. *Information to Applicants for Employment at Hoover Dam: Boulder Canyon Project*. Washington, D.C.: Bureau of Reclamation, 1931.

———. *The Story of Boulder Dam*. Conservation Bulletin no. 9. Washington, D.C.: U.S. Government Printing Office, 1941.

Van Dyke, Willard. "The Work of Ben Glaha." *Camera Craft* 42 (April 1935): 166–172.

Vrooman, Frank. "Uncle Sam's Romance with Science and the Soil." *Arena* 35 (January 1906): 36–46.

Water: Changing Values and Needs for People and Nature. Arlington, Va., and Washington, D.C.: National Water Resources Association and Bureau of Reclamation, n.d. (Pamphlet).

"'Water in the West' Honored." *Reclamation Era* 39 (May 1953): 107.

Webb, Robert H. *Grand Canyon, A Century of Change: Rephotography of the 1889–1890 Stanton Expedition*. Tucson: University of Arizona Press, 1996.

White, Graham J. *FDR and the Press*. Chicago: University of Chicago Press, 1979.

Wild, Peter. *Clarence King*. Boise, Idaho: Boise State University, 1981.

Wilkins, Thurman. *Clarence King: A Biography*. New York: Macmillan, 1958.

Williams, Albert N. *The Water and the Power: Development of the Five Great Rivers of the West*. New York: Duell, Sloan and Pearce, 1951.

Wilson, Richard Guy. *The Machine Age in America 1918–1941*. New York: Brooklyn Museum/Harry N. Abrams, 1986.

———. "Massive Deco Monument: The Enduring Strength of Boulder (Hoover) Dam." *AIA Journal* 72 (December 1983): 45–47.

Winfield, Betty Houchin. *FDR and the News Media*. Urbana and Chicago: University of Illinois Press, 1990.

Wolf, Donald E. *Big Dams and Other Dreams: The Six Companies Story*. Norman: University of Oklahoma Press, 1996.

Wolfe, Bertram D. *The Fabulous Life of Diego Rivera*. New York: Stein and Day, 1963.

Woodbury, David O. *The Colorado Conquest*. New York: Dodd, Mead, 1941.

Woollett, William. *California's Golden Age: With Illustrations and Text*. Santa Barbara, Calif.: Capra Press, 1989.

———. *Hoover Dam: Drawings, Etchings and Lithographs 1931–1933*. Los Angeles: Hennessey & Ingalls, 1986.

———. *Hoover Dam Project: A Complete Story of Its Construction in Picture Form from Lithographs & Sketches*. Los Angeles: Fred S. Lang, 1932.

Workers of the Writers' Program of the Work Project Administration in Northern California. *The Central Valley Project*. Sacramento: California State Department of Education, 1942.

Worster, Donald. *An Unsettled Country: Changing Landscapes of the American West*. Albuquerque: University of New Mexico Press, 1994.

ILLUSTRATION CREDITS

All photographs are black-and-white gelatin silver photographs. Photographs are by Ben Glaha unless otherwise noted.

Avery Architectural and Fine Arts Library, Columbia University in the City of New York
Empire State Building, New York City. Lewis W. Hine. 1930/1931.

Lewis Baltz
Foundation Construction, Many Warehouses, 2892 Kelvin, Irvine. Lewis Baltz. 1973–1974.

Bancroft Library
Truck Burning. Unattributed.
Wreck of Cars at Nevada Spillway. Unattributed.
Cableway. Unattributed.

Curtis Galleries, Minneapolis, Minn.
Conversation: Sky and Earth. Charles Sheeler. 1940. Oil on Canvas, 28 x 23 inches.

Robert Dawson
Cracked Mud and Vineyard, near Arvin, California. From the Great Central Valley Project. Robert Dawson. Copyright
        1985.

Library of Congress
Black Canyon Prior to Boulder Dam Construction (from an Old Print). B. D. Glaha (?). Lot 7365, LC-USZ62-114352. Lot
        7365 is the Ickes Portfolio; all of its prints are dated before 1935.
Cement Blending and Concrete Mixing Plants. Lot 7365, LC-USZ62-114357.
Interior of the Boulder Canyon Project Plant of the Babcock and Wilcox Company. Lot 7365, LC-USZ62-114364.
Workman with Water Bag. Lot 7365, LC-USZ-89645.
Nevada Desert Landscape near Boulder City. Lot 7365, LC-USZ62-114350.
Street Scene in Residential Section, Boulder City. Lot 7365, LC-USZ62-114351.
Blasting in Boulder Dam Abutment Excavations. Lot 7365, LC-USZ62-89649.
The Downstream Face of Boulder Dam as Seen from Lookout Point. Lot 7365, LC-USZ62-114359.

Steel Bar Reinforcement in Boulder Dam Intake Towers. Lot 7365, LC-USZ62-89657.

One of the Two Spillway Structures at Boulder Dam. Lot 7365, LC-USZ62-114361.

The Upstream Face of Boulder Dam During the Night Shift. Lot 7365, LC-USZ62-90539.

Rigger on Cableway Headtower During Construction. Lot 7365, LC-USZ62-89651.

Interior of Construction Cableway Headtower. Lot 7365, LC-USZ62-114353.

Boulder Dam Spillway Drum Gates and Piers. Lot 7365, LC-USZ62-114362.

Grouting Concrete Lining in Fifty-Foot-Diameter Diversion Tunnel. Lot 7365, LC-USZ62-114354.

The Nevada Intake Towers at Boulder Dam. Lot 7365, LC-USZ62-114360.

Lowering a 140-Ton Penstock Section into the Canyon over the 150-Ton-Capacity Cableway. Lot 7365, LC-USZ62-89658.

Life magazine

Fort Peck Dam, Montana. Margaret Bourke-White. 1936. First cover of *Life Magazine*, November 23, 1936. *Life* magazine
      copyright Time Inc. Reprinted with permission.

Museum of Fine Arts, Boston

View of Boulder Dam. Charles Sheeler. 1939.

Boulder Dam, Transmission Towers. Charles Sheeler. 1939.

Ingot Molds, Open Hearth Building—Ford Plant. Charles Sheeler. 1927.

Museum of Science and Industry

Down to Bedrock. 1932.

National Archives and Records Administration

Boulder Dam. Ansel Adams. 1941. 79-AAB-7.

Boulder Dam. Ansel Adams. 1942. 79-AAB-4.

Boulder Dam Power Units. Ansel Adams. 1941. 79-AAB-5.

Martin Stupich

Hoover Dam from Roadway, South into Boulder Canyon. Martin Stupich. 1989.

U.S. Department of the Interior, Bureau of Reclamation

Map of the Boulder Dam Area Showing the Principal Points of Scenic and Historical Interest. Undated drawing.
Ben Glaha.

The Dam as Seen from the Control Tower of the 150-Ton Cableway. December 30, 1933.

The Downstream Face of the Dam and a Portion of the Power Plant. October 2, 1934.

Horizontal View of Downstream Face of Boulder Dam and Power Plant. April 13, 1938.

Boulder Dam as Seen from High Point Upstream on Arizona Rim of Black Canyon. December 5, 1935.

Detail of Roof Slab and Beam Reinforcement in Canyon Wall Valve-House Structure. June 1, 1935.

Workmen Ascending Downstream Face of Dam on Skip Operating over Skids. March 16, 1934.

Eight-Cubic-Yard-Capacity Concrete Bucket Discharging Load in Dam Column Form. September 27, 1933.

Four-Cubic-Yard-Capacity Transit Mixer Discharging Concrete in Base of Downstream Nevada Intake Tower. November 5, 1933.

Chipping Backing-up Strip on Thirteen-Foot-Diameter Pipe Section, Babcock and Wilcox Plant. October 23, 1933.

Handling Thirty-Foot-Diameter Steel Penstock Pipe by Cableway. August 22, 1934.

Drillers at Work on Canyon Wall Above Power Plant Location. April 10, 1933.

The Millionth Cubic Yard of Concrete Is Placed in the Dam Forms. January 7, 1934.

Boulder Dam Consulting Board and Officials of the Bureau and Babcock and Wilcox in a Thirty-Foot-Diameter Penstock Pipe Section. January 15, 1935.

Looking Northward Across Escalante Plaza. October 19, 1933.

Government Administration Building, Boulder City. October 21, 1933.

North Section of Boulder City Showing Parked Area. July 27, 1934.

Abandoned and Dismantled Homesite at St. Thomas, Nevada. May 13, 1934.

View Looking Northeasterly across Reservoir Site from Observation Point. February 26, 1935.

Late Evening View at the Lower End of Grand Canyon Near Pierce's Ferry. November 7, 1935.

President Roosevelt Delivering Dedication Address. September 30, 1935.

The 200-Ton-Capacity La Crosse Trailer. July 16, 1934.

Riggers on Boom of Twelve-Ton Crane at Nevada Intake Towers. September 28, 1933.

Portion of 287.5 Kv. Transformers, Roof Take-off Structures for Units N-1 to N-4 Inclusive. April 12, 1938.

High Scalers Drilling into Canyon Wall 500 Feet above the Colorado River in Black Canyon. August 1, 1932.

Arizona Intake Towers as Seen from Surface of Reservoir. June 21, 1935.

Downstream Face of Dam Showing Powerhouse Footings. September 27, 1933.

Indians Employed as High Scalers. October 5, 1932.

Negroes Employed as Drillers. October 3, 1932.

Looking Upstream through the Upstream Tunnel Plug Construction in Diversion Tunnel No. 3. June 27, 1934.

Boulder Dam, a Portion of Intake Towers, the Rim Tower for Units N-1 to N-4. April 15, 1938.

The Crest of the Dam as Seen from the Arizona Abutment. September 17, 1936.

Bureau of Power and Light of Los Angeles Switchyard. April 15, 1938.

View Looking Upstream through the Nevada Spillway Channel from the Portal of the Inclined Tunnel. April 13, 1938.

Estate of William Woollett

Penstock Towers. William Woollett. Before 1935. Lithograph.

Diversion Tunnel Interior at Junction with Spillway Shaft. William Woollett. Before 1935. Lithograph.

General View Looking Upriver. William Woollett. Before 1935. Lithograph.

INDEX

ABOUT THE AUTHOR

Barbara Vilander received a Bachelor of Arts degree in psychology from the University of California at Santa Barbara, a Master of Arts degree in the history of art from the University of California at Santa Barbara, and a doctorate in the history of art and architecture from the University of California at Santa Barbara.